CW01494498

# THE
# TOP
# 200
# WEB SITES ON
# PERSONAL FINANCE

# The Top 200 Web Sites
# CD ROM + Guides

This series of interactive CD ROMs with accompanying Guides provides access to the *best quality* business information sites on the Net. Forget those hours of frustrating searching. Now the work has been done for you. Illustra's team of researchers has spent countless hours scrutinizing thousands of Web sites to select only those that are truly relevant and useful to your specific needs.

Available so far in this new series:

- The Top 200 Web Sites on E-Commerce
- The Top 200 Web Sites for Marketing
- The Top 200 Web Sites for Personal Finance
- The Top 200 Web Sites for Small Business

Each CD ROM features:

- fast access to the selected sites;
- a fully featured Web browser;
- free online information updates.

Each accompanying Guide gives general advice on how to make best use of the Internet as an information resource, and detailed descriptions and ratings of each selected site.

Designed to save busy people valuable time and money, each CD ROM and Guide together provide a powerful interactive business tool.

# THE
# TOP
# 200
# WEB SITES ON
# PERSONAL FINANCE

## Christina Daniels

INSTITUTE OF DIRECTORS

KOGAN
PAGE

First published in 2000

Apart from any fair dealing for the purposes of research or private study, or criticism or review, as permitted under the Copyright, Designs and Patents Act 1988, this publication may only be reproduced, stored or transmitted, in any form or by any means, with the prior permission in writing of the publishers, or in the case of reprographic reproduction in accordance with the terms and licences issued by the CLA. Enquiries concerning reproduction outside these terms should be sent to the publishers at the undermentioned address:

Kogan Page Limited
120 Pentonville Road
London N1 9JN
UK

Kogan Page US
163 Central Avenue, Suite 2
Dover NH 03820
USA

© Illustra Research Ltd, 2000

The right of Illustra Research Ltd to be identified as the author of this work has been asserted by them in accordance with the Copyright, Designs and Patents Act 1988.

This book has been endorsed by the Institute of Directors.

The endorsement is given to selected Kogan Page books which the IoD recognizes as being of specific interest to its members and providing them with up-to-date, informative and practical resources for creating business success. Kogan Page books endorsed by the IoD represent the most authoritative guidance available on a wide range of subjects including management, finance, marketing, training and HR.

The views expressed in this book are those of the author and are not necessarily the same as those of the Institute of Directors.

**British Library Cataloguing in Publication Data**

A CIP record for this book is available from the British Library.

ISBN 0 7494 3270 5

Typeset by Saxon Graphics Ltd, Derby
Printed and bound in Great Britain by Bell & Bain Ltd, Glasgow

Christina Daniels works for the BBC as a researcher. She is also a freelance author who has written and researched extensively on personal-finance matters, and has contributed to a number of publications in both the UK and Brazil.

# Contents

*Contents*

*1*

# Explore personal finance Web sites with this guide

Search for the best mortgage from several dozen providers without trudging around the High Street or spending time on 'hold' during phone calls; browse for the best credit-card deal without enduring a barrage of sales pitch; choose your bank account without stepping outside your house. Because they offer these benefits, personal finance Web sites are among the major growth areas on the Internet.

The financial services marketplace is changing radically, with both the entry of new providers and the development of innovative new delivery channels. The Internet is becoming increasingly important in this fast-changing world. Its interactive potential makes it an exciting channel for delivering personalized financial services, and the Web is a powerful information tool, giving potential customers more choice and freedom to identify which services they want to use, and which provider offers the right deal.

Whether you're a beginner wanting to learn some finance basics, or you're itching to become a seasoned online investor, getting to grips with what's available on the Internet is a must for anyone interested in personal finance.

From this guide you can expect:

■ Fast access (via the CD ROM) to high-quality personal finance Web sites.

- A critical overview of current personal finance Web sites and pointers that will help you become more Internet literate.

- A guide that concentrates on the **content** of Web sites, and is not obsessed by the technology.

- Tips on how to get more from the Internet as an information resource.

- A guide that focuses on using the World Wide Web (WWW), although you will find a section on e-mail and newsgroups.

What you won't get from this book:

- A manual that will tell you how to become a personal finance expert. If you want that sort of guide, put this book down **now**! The Top 200 series guides offer an overview of what information resources you can expect to find **on the Internet** in a particular subject area. The guides won't instruct you in the subject but will give you access to a range of useful Web sites from which you will be able to learn a great deal.

- Any pretence that every personal finance Web site that ever existed has been scoured in the process of writing this book. That's about as realistic as someone claiming to have catalogued and read every book in the world. Thousands of Web sites have been evaluated in the process of compiling this book, and every title undergoes the rigorous research process outlined below. We can guarantee that each guide features a hand-picked selection of Web sites that you will find useful.

- Detailed instructions on how to build your own cracking personal finance Web site. Our aim is to promote the Web as an information resource, and the guide is therefore aimed at people who want to improve their Web skills and learn more about useful Web sites in their particular area of interest.

Don't think this guide is going to stay up to date unless you regularly update it. We've all heard the clichés about a day being a long time on the Net. It's certainly true that what is currently available on the Internet will have changed within a couple of months. Once you have bought the guide, updates can be easily obtained by visiting the Illustra Research Web site. Check it out for yourself by clicking the Illustra button within the guide.

## How we select and rate the Top 200 Web sites in this guide

Illustra Research has devised its own procedures to locate, select and evaluate Web sites, and the same criteria are applied for each guide in the Top 200 series. We have examined a wide range of methodologies that other people, often university librarians, have devised to judge the quality of information on the Internet, and have incorporated these into our own system.

All the reviewed and rated Web sites in this book have been individually examined and measured against our twin criteria, **relevance** and **ease of use**. We use these criteria to present a shortlist of the very best sites our team of authors and researchers have found over months of searching and evaluation.

Our main principle is the extent to which a Web site does or does not meet the needs of a particular group of users. We are not trying to establish a universal quality standard, or a 'Good Housekeeping seal of approval'. We have designed our system of selection and evaluation in order to present sites that we think our target group of users is going to find valuable as sources of information.

But can you trust our judgements? Doesn't any review or rating system in the end depend on personal taste? How can a star rating sum up the value of a Web site? Responding to these concerns we have developed a two-step method for identifying sites worth sharing. Our authors have employed this evaluation process and we include details to show how demanding we have been when choosing the sites for the Top 200 series guides.

# Step one: establishing threshold criteria

With thousands of potential sites to sift through we established our baseline for inclusion. Using our two criteria, relevance and ease of use, we designed a checklist of those attributes a Web site must possess before we consider recommending it.

### Relevance

Here we think about the accuracy and credibility of the site's content. Is the purpose and scope of the site clear, or does it have a hidden agenda? Does the site undergo regular updates or revisions? Is there a physical address, or at least a phone number, to confirm the existence in the real world of those responsible for the site? Does the site present information in a way that is sensitive to what our particular group of users is likely to want?

### Ease of use

Here we look at the design and the navigation facilities. We consider how friendly they are for a newcomer to the Web – someone short of time but hungry for information. What is the general appearance of the site? Is the text easy to read? Are the links appropriate and well described? We think that interactivity is essential for an effective site, you should be able to ask questions, carry out transactions and generally use the information in a more active way that simply reading words off a screen. So the sites we rate highly offer much more than simply an e-mail address for communication with their users.

# Step two: awarding a star rating

The star rating for relevance and ease of use provides a quick guide to what the site offers. Sites that satisfy our criteria are measured on a scale of one to five. Here we distinguish what is good, what is better and what is truly outstanding. The key to the ratings is listed here in full.

## Relevance

✪ This site offers basic information of use to the intended audience for the guide.

✪✪ This site provides some useful information plus some expert insight or value.

✪✪✪ A comprehensive site with authoritative information and resources.

✪✪✪✪ An excellent, authoritative site with features that make it an indispensable tool.

✪✪✪✪✪ The very best of its kind to be found at present. A 'must see'.

## Ease of use

✪ An accessible, easy to navigate interface with limited interactive features.

✪✪ An interface with some interactive features that enrich user experience.

✪✪✪ An interface that conveys a high level of design and usability in most areas.

✪✪✪✪ An interface that conveys a high level of design and usability in all areas.

✪✪✪✪✪ The best in its class – redefines the current standard of excellence.

A one-star rating for relevance indicates that the site is well worth a visit for basic information, some of which may be unique to the organization that runs it and will not be found elsewhere. As each of our guides is aimed at a particular group of users, all the sites they recommend have a value; if we have found a site that we think is useful, then it will be in the guide. For this reason there are no zero scores for relevance in *The Top 200 Web Sites for Personal Finance* – what would be the point? Some sites may have a zero score for ease of use however. In such cases the standard of information contained on the site compensates for the site's poor design. We trust that in time, perhaps even by the time you visit the site, improvements will have been made and its usability will match the standard of its content.

Rapid change is one of the Web's greatest strengths as an information source and we appreciate that sites can alter between visits. We are committed to constantly reviewing and re-evaluating the contents of our guides. For this reason all our reviews carry the date the site was assessed. A site that is regularly updated and has satisfied our demand for accuracy, credibility and usability should, by its nature, maintain a high standard. But your comments and contributions are invaluable. If you think our reviews don't match your views, it may be because the site has changed, so please do let us know – visit the Illustra Web site by clicking the Illustra button. If you've found a site you think we should include, click on **My Sites**.

# 2

# Using the Internet

## So what's all the fuss about?

The rise of the Internet is seemingly unstoppable. Media coverage reminds us daily that the Internet and the Web are going to transform how people live and do business. We are urged to go online and get Internet literate. Bookshops are adorned with guides to becoming 'Net savvy' – but have *you* wondered what all the fuss is about? Have *you* noticed that using the Internet can be disappointing or a positively frustrating experience?

The Internet for many people is an **information jungle**, and the sheer scale of information available is overwhelming. Search engines are crude and inadequate tools for information searching, since no quality assurance system operates. Most searches made with search engines return a vast number of Web sites, with no guarantee that the information turned up will be useful or relevant.

Neither consumers nor business users have time or money to waste doing this sort of thankless searching. What *you* need is access to high-quality Web sites oriented to the individual's specific needs. However, when you use the Web, you end up 'ploughing' through thousands of largely irrelevant search results; it's like being given an unreliable and gargantuan guide to the world when you just want solid and dependable information about a weekend break in Lisbon.

To make it worse, half the sites you come across are appalling, out of date or 'under construction'. How many businesses do you know who would mail out a sales brochure with blank pages saying 'not yet written'? There is no quality control or equivalent of 'refuse disposal' on the Web, and again and again you will come across 'detritus' sites, created and then abandoned, filled with inaccurate and incomplete information. Using the Web feels more like 'grubbing around' in a skip than being on an information super-highway, and you can easily waste half the morning on unsuccessful Internet searches. So what *is* all the fuss about?

# The value of the Internet

Despite these difficulties, there *is* useful information available on the Web, which *can* save users time and money. For example, did you know that British users can currently use the Web, without payment, to do all of the following:

- check phone bills and amend discount offers;
- print out detailed street maps of anywhere in the UK by typing in a postcode;
- set up e-mail groups enabling them to keep in contact with other people who don't share a computer network with them;
- compare house prices, crime rates or council tax bills with other areas or the national average;
- compare water, gas and electricity bills with what they might have paid with a different supplier;
- find businesses, UK phone numbers, UK post codes, company information – all for free!

Apart from these 'essentials' that anyone will find useful (which are of course all in the guide), there is specific information out there relevant to your needs. Whether you need to know about employment law, job vacancies, training opportunities, stock market quotations or information about export markets, there is often timely information that can be much easier to obtain than it is in print – provided you know where to look. But it takes time and some degree of familiarity with the Web to locate these useful sites.

# User driven, not technology driven

The solid research behind the guides is based on a clear under-standing of how the Internet works as channel of communication and information, not just as a technology. You will have already found that most guides to the Internet tell you more than you ever want to know about the technology, but less than you need to know about what is out there. The guides in the Top 200 series tell you how to *use* the technology, and they focus on the specific needs of groups of users. For example, we know the Internet is good for British users for the following reasons:

# Essential benefits of the Internet – a summary

- The Internet provides access to a wealth of up-to-date information from a variety of sources, which can be invaluable when information changes quickly, or when comparisons need to be made, eg for purchasing.

- The Internet is a cost-effective channel for communication, especially in global terms.

- It provides a good way to network that goes far beyond one's physical geographic reach.

- It gives small companies the opportunity to compete on the same footing as larger companies, since they can sell on a global scale without the large overheads of a shop-front presence or having to embark on costly paper-based marketing campaigns.

- The interactive features of the Web can be used to create more sophisticated and attractive product delivery channels for consumers, eg through providing searchable databases on product lines or by providing links to other sites. This benefits vendors *and* consumers.

- It offers access to free, good-quality information that can't be obtained as easily or as conveniently from other sources.

## How can good-quality information be free on the Web?

This is because many organizations have jumped on the online bandwagon but haven't as yet worked out how to make people pay for this information. On commercial sites revenue is usually acquired by following an advertising model, and because they want to attract people, and therefore keep advertisers happy, they offer services and features including free information that they hope will pull in visitors. This *may* change with the development of new kinds of online payment systems, but at the moment it makes much of the free information on the Web extremely valuable – if you can find it, of course.

The other reason why valuable information is available on the Web without charge is that many of the information providers are governmental or non-profit-making bodies. They offer information as part of their responsibilities to the public.

## Why you shouldn't ignore the Internet

One reason why it is currently difficult to locate good-quality sites is that hype and excitement about the Web has led to companies and organizations rushing to 'get online'. Consequently many current sites have no obvious value or usefulness and have been thrown up by companies desperate to carve out a Web presence. They are created without enough consideration or awareness as to what makes a valuable or useful site, and are often ill-conceived or poorly-designed 'corporate brochures', so it is not surprising that their pages are frustrating to users (see Chapter 3).

However, as the technology matures, and the use and design of Web sites becomes more sophisticated, it is likely that many of the more hopeless ones will get 'weeded out', and Internet users will become more adept at recognizing styles and categories of sites. These more literate Internet users will have significant advantages over those individuals who have shunned the Internet because they think it is full of rubbish, and have yet to acquire any familiarity with it. Since the Internet is here to stay, some degree of Internet literacy is necessary just to be able to operate in the new channels of communication and information that have been created by the Web.

## Key points

- Don't ignore the Internet because you think it'll go away – it won't!
- Don't allow yourself to be swayed or panicked by the hype.
- Recognize the strengths of the Internet as well as its weaknesses.
- Use this guide to begin to make yourself more Internet literate.

## How we deal with commercial sites or vendors

In this book and on the CD ROM, you will find reviews of vendors' sites in a range of product areas. These sites have been included because they are good examples of their kind (eg e-commerce-enabled sites), or they may offer information or additional features that set them aside from other vendors' sites of their type. Most straightforward commercial sites, which use the Internet solely as a promotional medium (and are described in Chapter 3 as 'corporate brochure' sites), have **not** been included in this book. For example, we have made no attempt to include a complete listing of the Web sites of, say, firms who repair computers. One reason is that, if you live in Ashford, it will not help you to have to 'wade' through sites of firms in Barnsley. Another is that there are good sites *on the Internet* that do exactly this. You may have heard of Yahoo! or Yellow Pages, but have you heard of Scoot? (see Business essentials, on page 66.)

Wherever possible we have tried to find sites that help you to find the commercial products and services you are looking for. 'Corporate brochure' sites perform a valuable function if you are sure you want information about that company and they provide it. What the Internet does really well is deliver up-to-the-minute information from the databases that lie behind the Web sites. We have included directories of vendors that are comprehensive, easily searchable and maintained on a daily or weekly basis. We have excluded those 'directories' where firms included have to pay, and those that are patchy in coverage, are not maintained, or are impossibly difficult to use.

# 3

# Web site types – a user's guide

We have all learnt to recognize types of television programmes – what a documentary looks like, for example, as opposed to a soap opera, or what to expect from the 'Nine O'Clock News' – but it is not quite so easy with Web sites. The Internet is a new medium and Web sites often cross over several forms and styles, borrowing from newspapers, advertising and television amongst many others. What's more, they are changing all the time.

However, there *are* recognizable characteristics that can help you identity what to expect from a Web site. Getting familiar with these signs can help you pinpoint what type of Web page you've just 'stumbled' on to and help you establish quickly whether it is going to be of any use to you. Read on for an introduction to the fascinating art of Web site spotting…

## Seven types of Web site

### Type one: the 'corporate brochure'

These are the spectacularly boring efforts of a company that has usually just taken the text and images from their corporate brochure and put them online.

You will often find that these sites were constructed in a fit of enthusiasm by firms who had just discovered the Web, and who thought they should have a Web presence. They had no clue about why or what they should 'do' with it. In most cases, they simply transferred their promotional literature on to their Web site. Now they wonder why no one ever visits it.

As a consequence of this failure, and the subsequent loss of initial enthusiasm, these sites can fall into a state of chronic disrepair with little updating or maintenance. Others are updated but remain tedious.

You can recognize these sites by the fact they look like corporate brochures – typically the home page will feature glossy photographs or logos, and it is always the same thing on the 'menu' – pages on Services (sales pitch) About Us (historically slanted sales pitch) and Products (relentless full-frontal sales pitch). You won't find e-commerce on a corporate brochure site, or any interactive features. You may be lucky and find an e-mail address, but don't be surprised if you don't get a reply when you use it.

You won't find any examples of true 'corporate brochures' in the guide – they didn't satisfy our criteria for what makes a site useful. But we have included 'corporate brochures' that offer something other than promoting their own products (such as the insurance sites introduced in Chapter 8). Also, you will find directory sites with links to many of the 'corporate brochure' sites. If you want specific information about a particular company they can be useful.

## Type two: the 'labour of love'

The amateurish layout, the background that makes it hard to read the text, even the use of standard clipart are all characteristics of a 'labour of love' Web site, usually created by an individual who is an obsessive enthusiast and wants to share his or her passion or knowledge with the rest of the world. These individuals collect links to absolutely everything they can find on the Internet, and sometimes add their own comments to the lists of links.

Whilst most 'labours of love' are the work of hobbyists, you will come across business-oriented Internet sites that are 'labours of love' and they *can* be very useful and informative. You need to exercise your discretion and decide for yourself. Often, like many works of art, 'labours of love' are left unfinished or are even abandoned, so don't presume the material presented is up to date or even accurate.

The following site, which deals with cryptography, is an example of a labour of love that is genuinely useful to an e-commerce specialist with a deep interest in security matters.

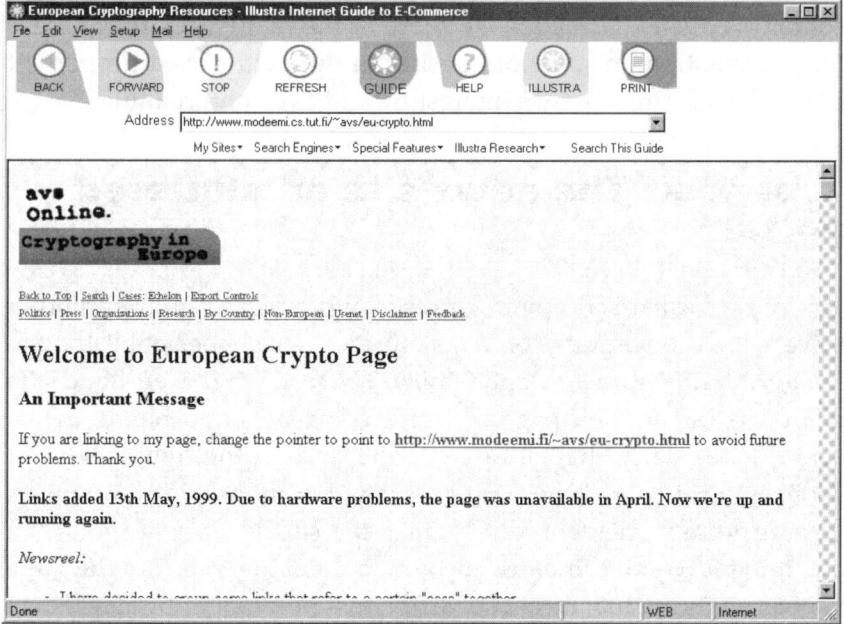

# Type three: The 'flashy Flash' sites

The supreme example of the triumph of style over content, 'flashy Flash' sites tend to be hosted or created by designers or new media consultancies who want to show off their use of new media technologies (especially Macromedia's Flash animation package). Look out for intricate graphics, fancy dissolves and all things animated. The giveaway for spotting a 'flashy Flash' site is a home page with something running across the screen for no obvious reason.

'Flashy Flash' sites can be bandwidth-hungry and tediously slow to download if you are working on a slow connection via a dial-up modem, or during peak use times. The best of these sites should give you the option to switch off the animation and some will require plug-ins (such as Shockwave) before you can even get into them.

We've no examples of this type in the guide. They didn't meet our criteria because the technology intrudes so much that the content is pushed aside (or not there in the first place). But there *is* Flash animation on some of the sites in the guide; used properly it can make informative sites interesting and even entertaining.

## Type four: The news site or 'cluttered portal'

The news format is becoming increasingly popular on the Internet since it uses conventions of magazine and newspaper publishing to make Web sites attractive and familiar to users. On the left-hand side of the news site Web page is typically a navigation menu, in the centre is regularly changed news copy, and on the right is a list of sponsors or links to other editions or publications. Using the news format prompts readers to recognize the site as a publication with changing text, and therefore encourage them to re-visit (in the same way as an individual might subscribe to a newspaper or magazine). News sites are often produced by offline publishers (such as the *Financial Times*) and focus on a specific interest area (as ZDNet does) or audience (as a trade journal would).

News sites can be well designed and pleasant to use. However, over-excitable site designers can try to stick too many menu options or links on them – hence the 'cluttered portal' phenomenon – a serious trial for the eyes. This problem is further magnified when 8 pt type has been used by a designer in a effort to squeeze as much text into as small a space as possible.

News sites tend to be more useful if you want to browse in a particular subject area than when you have a particular query or piece of information to look up. However, some people don't like browsing Internet sites and prefer to use paper publications, so it is really down to you to try out news sites for yourself.

## Type five: the 'cunningly concealed commercial'

Like promotional features in magazines that ape the editorial layout of their 'host', these Web sites are trying to sell you something, but are pretending that is not their main purpose. Common examples include Web sites presented as 'information resources' or 'directories', but you either have to pay to use them, the entries in the 'directory' are actually paid adverts, or the 'resources' are trying to sell you the services of a consultant.

A quick way to spot the 'cunningly concealed commercial' is to go to the About Us section on the home page and find out who has created and maintains the site. You shouldn't necessarily reject this sort of site but we all like to know where we stand. We have rejected them for the Top 200 series, but we have included some commercial sites that offer genuinely useful information *in addition to* a sales pitch.

## Type six: the 'dull but worthy' site

Mostly produced by public bodies, such as a trade association or your local council, these sites usually provide useful information but often give little thought to making accessing them a pleasurable or even straightforward process for their victim (the user).

Whilst the best can be accessible and sensibly organized, the worst will tell you what they do via a clunky and badly designed interface. Even more deadly is some public body sites' tendency to feature huge numbers of very boring documents on obscure aspects of their regulatory or legislative procedure presented as pages and pages of dense text. The more advanced of these will allow you to download their documents, sometimes in PDF format, for which you need the (free) Adobe Acrobat reader installed.

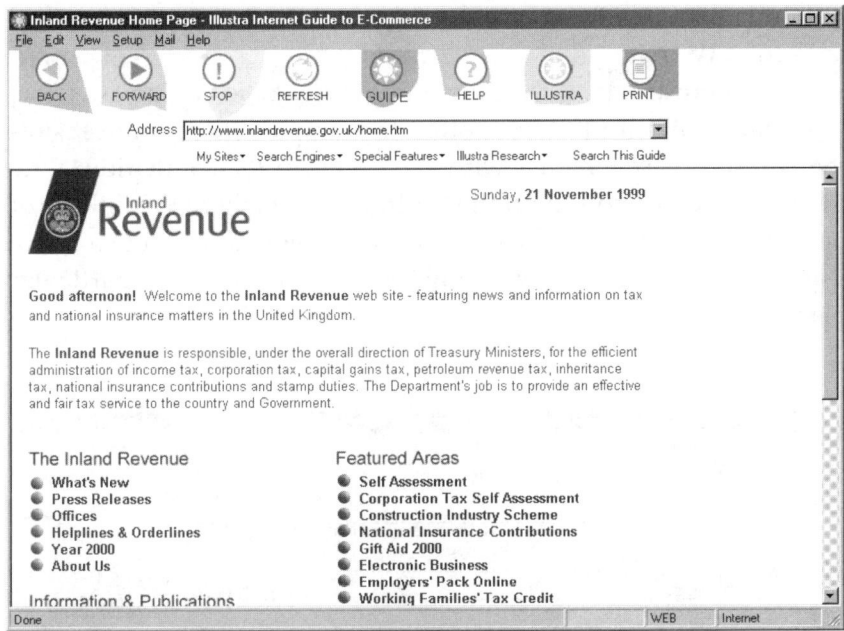

However, public Web sites are often useful as a first port of call when you need to deal with a particular agency (see the highly-recommended Inland Revenue site featured above) but public organizations often lack the resources and/or imagination to develop truly innovative sites.

## Type seven: the 'firm favourite'

These Web sites are sheer pleasure to use. They come in all shapes and sizes, but they are the ones you return to again and again. 'Firm favourites' usually exploit the interactive potential of the Web to the full. They are innovative, imaginative and offer something that really meets the needs of Internet users. On them you will find searchable databases, delivered via well-designed and intuitive interfaces. They provide access to features, services and information that cannot be easily found elsewhere *on* or even *off* the Web. It is this combination of excellent, fully interactive design *and* high-quality, genuinely useful information that makes a 'firm favourite' Web site.

Interestingly, it isn't just big players who can create these top-quality sites. In fact, it is often the simpler, more modest sites that exploit a clever idea with most flair and imagination. One example of this is found on the Multimap site where the linking of postcodes to online mapping makes it possible to provide a really useful service to anyone wanting to give directions to a particular place.

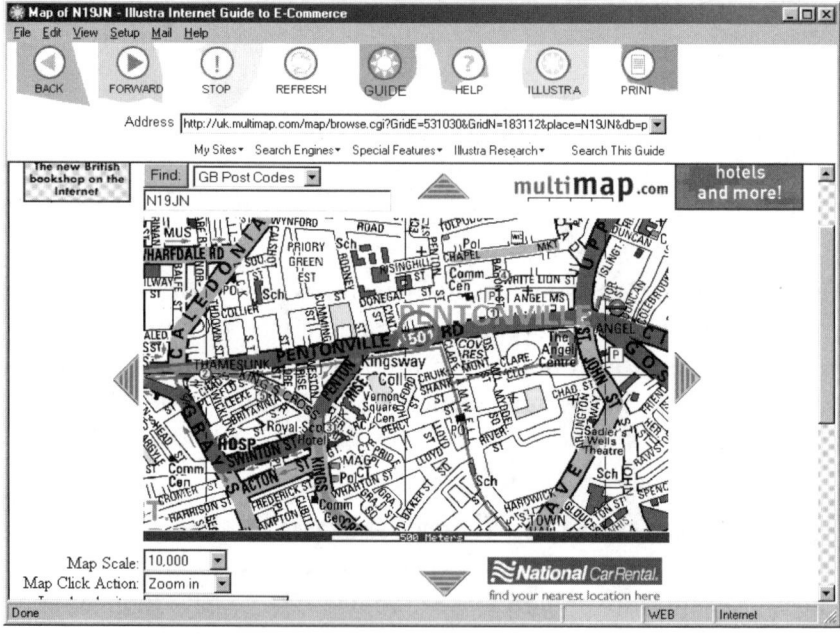

Sadly, 'firm favourites' are a rare occurrence on the Web at present. We can only hope that as Web site developers become more clued up, 'firm favourites' will become more common than the welcome exception. You will find such sites strongly featured in Business essentials (see pages 66–72).

# 4

# Beyond the Web: e-mail and newsgroups

The hype around the Internet usually focuses upon the wonders of the World Wide Web, wowing us with 'cool' Web sites, the lure of e-commerce and the promised link-up with digital TV. But there are other tools available through the Net and it is worth spending a moment considering their potential value before dashing off to surf the flashy attractions.

## E-mail is easy

With the spotlight on 'dot.com' companies these days, e-mail seems very much the poor relation of the Internet. Yet it is a fantastically flexible tool. It is cheap to use, easy to understand and has a lot of hidden abilities. Having been around for 30 years (since the birth of the Net) it's not subject to some of the technical changes that might force you to update your Web browser every three months.

For many people e-mail is the best reason for being on the Internet. It is a cheap, convenient means of communicating, whether it's across the office or around the globe. It can be used to keep in touch with people who are asleep when you're awake, to share news and information with hundreds of people at the same time, and to gain access to specialist information. It is rapidly becoming an essential tool, sitting neatly alongside the phone, letters and face-to-face meetings as part of the way to get things done.

# Are you getting the most from your e-mail?

Whatever you think of the Internet, it is becoming increasingly difficult to avoid the use of e-mail. Anyone who can use a word processor can compose a message and send it to one, twenty or ten thousand people at the press of a button.

Despite fears about the growth of viruses and junk mail, the volume of e-mail traffic is expanding even faster than the Net in general. With the rising convergence of e-mail with mobile phones and faxes, this expansion can only increase.

## One-to-one e-mail

The starting point for e-mail is usually to see it as a substitute for an answerphone. I send you a message, which you receive when you check your mailbox. You compose a reply and send it back, so that I can pick it up when I next check my mail. It is an *asynchronous* means of communicating that has many benefits over the spoken word.

For a start, most people tend not to write in the same way that they speak. We tend to use whole sentences, for example, comprising complete words, and consider our message more carefully before committing it to paper, so a written message can often be clearer and more logically constructed than a spoken one. This helps both parties enormously. Replies can be more considered when you don't have to think instantly as you do on the telephone.

If I write you an e-mail, you can include my words in your reply. There is no need to spend ages explaining exactly what you're replying to, when you can copy my question back to me followed by a simple 'yes' or 'no'. You may want to copy my words into a word-processing document, or make some other use of it, without having to type anything yourself. You can forward it to someone else at a stroke, or copy others in on an exchange with a mutual colleague or friend.

Of course a quick telephone call can be far more productive than a series of disjointed e-mails, and a chat over a pint is usually far more conducive to reaching an agreement than struggling to type with one finger. But as an option for one-to-one communication it offers advantages over phone, faxes and meetings that should not be underestimated.

## One-to-many e-mail

The penetration of e-mail has created a huge impetus for communicating with lots of people in one go. The cost advantages over traditional mailing options are overwhelming, and the economy of scale is mind-blowing. Why send one message to one person by post for 20p when for about 5p (the current BT minimum charge) you can go online and send an e-mail to hundreds of people and for 10p send it to thousands?

## 'Spam'

The Internet community has long known of the potential benefits of mass mailing and has recognized that it also has the potential to drown the Internet in a tide of e-mail. Because it is so difficult to regulate anything online, it has been left to Internet users themselves to seek to control the use of 'spam' – the name coined for the use of unsolicited e-mail sent to hundreds or thousands of people at the same time, usually through a mailing list or newsgroup that somebody else has created. It should be distinguished from targeted e-mail sent to a mailing list that *you or your company* have created.

If you need to know more about a term like 'spam' – and whether it did indeed originate from that Monty Python sketch – you can make use of the Writing aids section in Business essentials (see pages 70–71). The invaluable *Webopedia* also helps you out:

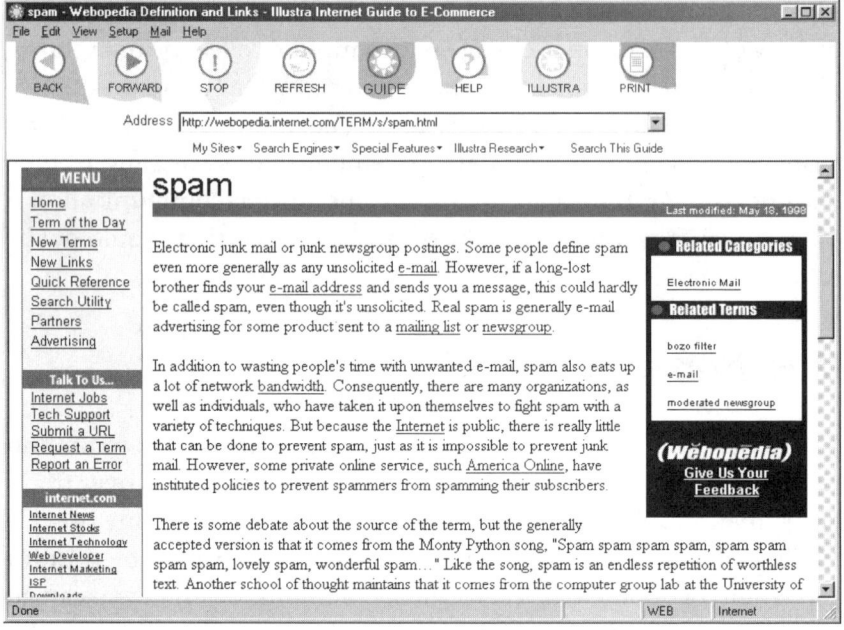

Many direct-marketing professionals view e-mail as manna from heaven, and list brokers have traded in e-mail addresses for many years. As with a lot of such tactics, most people only use them because they are successful and there are plenty of Web sites that explain how they work, and how to integrate e-mail mailings with other marketing tools.

## Is free e-mail worth it?

The number of people with e-mail has escalated sharply in the past year or so, partly due to free services such as Hotmail. These services are usually accessed through a Web page and make it possible to get and send messages anywhere that you can log on to the Net. The phenomenal growth of cybercafés in such traveller-friendly destinations as Thailand and Australia is testament to how convenient such services can be when you're on the move.

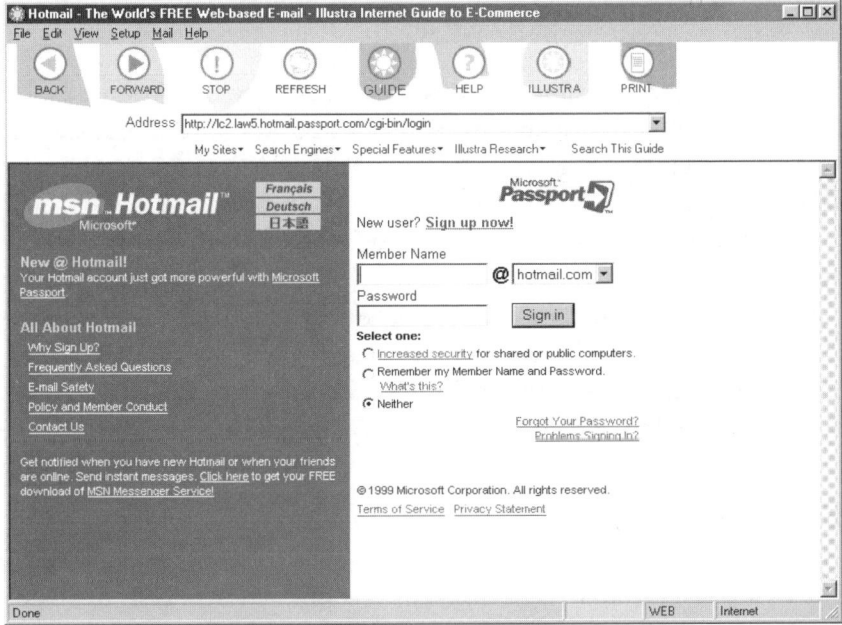

Free systems are great for personal use (whereas most business people will be looking for something slightly different, both in terms of security and the desire to link e-mail in with their overall online presence).

## Many-to-many e-mail

This type of e-mail communication is becoming recognized by many in the Net-literate community as an important part of building relationships with contacts. You can send customized e-mails and contacts can e-mail you *and each other* to take part in online discussions. You can use a free service (such as eGroups) or you can buy software to build this capability into your Web site.

# Newsgroups

Newsgroups are considered a nether region of the Internet, not usually travelled by the average Internet punter and populated by mythological Internet gurus who swap hackers' codes, dirty pictures and inane gossip. This is all true, but there is more to it than that.

Somewhere in your e-mail package or Web browser you'll have 'stumbled' across something to do with newsgroups, or have read of them in magazines or an Internet guidebook. It is very easy to ignore them as it requires a bit of work to get the best out of them, but you may find pearls of wisdom, new contacts or the answer to a technical question, which makes it all worthwhile.

## This is not news

The first point is that newsgroups are not full of news. They are electronic forums that discuss specific topics, identified by a name such as uk.jobs.wanted, alt.biz.misc, or even alt.recovery.cow-fetish. Anyone can post a message to a forum, and everyone subscribed to it will receive it. Everyone else in the group can then see any reply to the message.

At its simplest a newsgroup is a straightforward discussion tool, enabling people with similar interests to ask questions, share information and swap gossip. There may be a group relating to the trade you're in, a country you're interested in, or a piece of software you're having problems with.

There are some 25,000 of those groups out there, running through a piece of technology called Usenet. The whole thing is e-mail based, and to join the discussion you need to be subscribed to a group. Netscape's and Microsoft's browser packages include software for reading newsgroups, but it does take a bit of setting up for the beginner.

Another route into the world of newsgroups is the amazing www.deja.com. This site catalogues the messages on nearly every newsgroup, and has archives going back to 1995 on some lists. It has a search facility to help track down useful groups, and lots of other add-ons to link you into related stuff. It has recently become more of a portal to consumers, but you can still find what you want from newsgroups if you 'dig deep'.

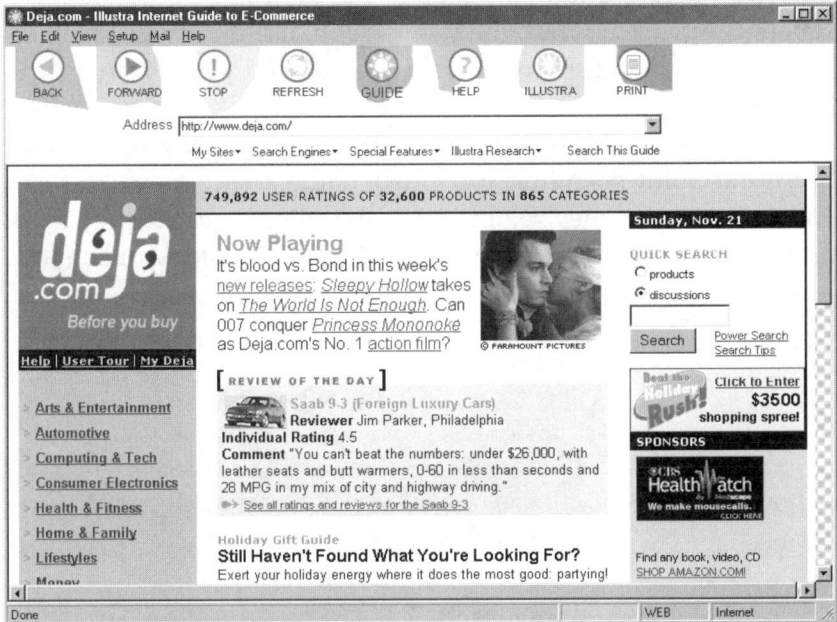

## Using newsgroups

Newsgroups are not for everyone. They can seem difficult to use and often appear to be inhabited by people who are either too knowledgeable or just too intimidating to deal with. But they could be a great source of help and many people swear by them for up-to-the minute interaction with others anywhere in the world.

Specialist newsreader software is available to help make reading easy and you can download messages when you check your e-mail. They can be delivered with your regular e-mail, or browsed online. You can keep tabs on any number of lists by using the software to subscribe to them, and either check them as they come in or leave half an hour aside now and then to read back through recent messages.

To find the best list for you, go to www.deja.com and start searching for subjects. Many newsgroups relate to recreational activity, so serious information can be hard to come by at first. Have a good 'rummage around' the site, though, use the search facilities, think laterally, join lists you like the look of, and you'll soon get the hang of it.

Newsgroups are not the user-friendliest of technologies and there's no point spending frustrated hours trying to make them work for you. But they're obviously only there because they work for millions of people, and it's just possible they could work for you.

# 5

# Personal finance and the Internet

## Introduction

Personal finance Web sites are becoming one of the most popular reasons why people go online. You can now open and manage your bank account online, invest in shares while accessing in-depth industry information previously only available to brokers, and receive quotes for your mortgage, insurance or loan.

The Web is making it possible for service providers to offer features that would have been far too expensive to include in the High Street branch, while saving further money by reducing the need for new branches and call centres. In addition, the technology allows Web site providers to offer individuals highly personalized services on demand.

You can save money and time by using Web sites and organizing your finances online – you just need to know where to start. There are plenty of badly designed and uninformative Web sites out there, and trying to sort the wheat from the chaff can be a time-consuming and largely irritating experience. You're probably familiar with typing a term into a search engine then being faced with a few thousand results, none of which seem to be what you were looking for in the first place. You will not do this when searching for information on personal finance, as our extensive research has provided you with *The Top 200 Web Sites for Personal Finance.*

To get the maximum value from this book, install the accompanying CD ROM on your PC and access the sites direct from the guide. Log on to the Illustra Research Web site by clicking the Illustra button, and you'll find you can keep your guide up to date. This is important, because the Internet is developing rapidly. We will have discovered new personal finance Web sites by the time you read this and you'll want to know about them.

# More details about this guide

This is not an expert guide to personal finance like those found on the shelves of any bookshop. It is, rather, an expert guide to what's on offer on the Internet for those interested in personal finance. The difference is important: we take you to useful sites, but you must make up your own mind before you follow the advice you find. Illustra Research does not endorse the products or services on any of the sites in the Top 200, and you should think of taking professional advice before parting with any money. If you want an independent financial adviser, some of the sites here can help you find one.

In the following chapters you will find sections relating to each topic covered in the guide, and the complete list of Web addresses (URLs) from the CD ROM. We provide some case studies showing you how you can make effective use of the guide. *The Top 200 Web Sites for Personal Finance* covers all your basic personal finance needs, from managing your bank account online to finding the most competitive rate for household insurance. The Internet can be overwhelming, but if you work with the Web sites in the guide first, you'll find the range and depth of information easier to manage. You can always go beyond the sites contained here, either through links from the pages that come up, or by using a search engine. Click on Search Engines in the guide to get quickly to the most popular ones.

You'll find that the majority of the sites we've included in this book are specific to the UK. We've left out most American personal finance sites because we feel they will not easily pop pop to the needs of a British consumer.

---

**Top Tip – filtering out US sites**

The Internet is still dominated by US sites and avoiding them can be a difficult task. Commercial sites whose addresses end in '.com' are generally US-based, but this is not always the case. A useful hint when searching for UK specific sites is to include 'UK' at the end of your search term.

---

# What to look out for

The best finance-related sites contain highly useful features such as interactive calculators, online quotes and rate-comparison charts, offering information that you'd be hard pressed to find so easily elsewhere. In the sites included in the guide you'll find interactive calculators that work out the contents insurance of your home, what type of mortgage you're eligible for, how much you can borrow from a personal loan and more. You'll have access to online quotes for insurance cover and a mortgage, and rate-comparison tables that tell you which companies offer the best deal.

A good example comes from **Paragon Mortgages** (see Mortgages – Resources, page 90).

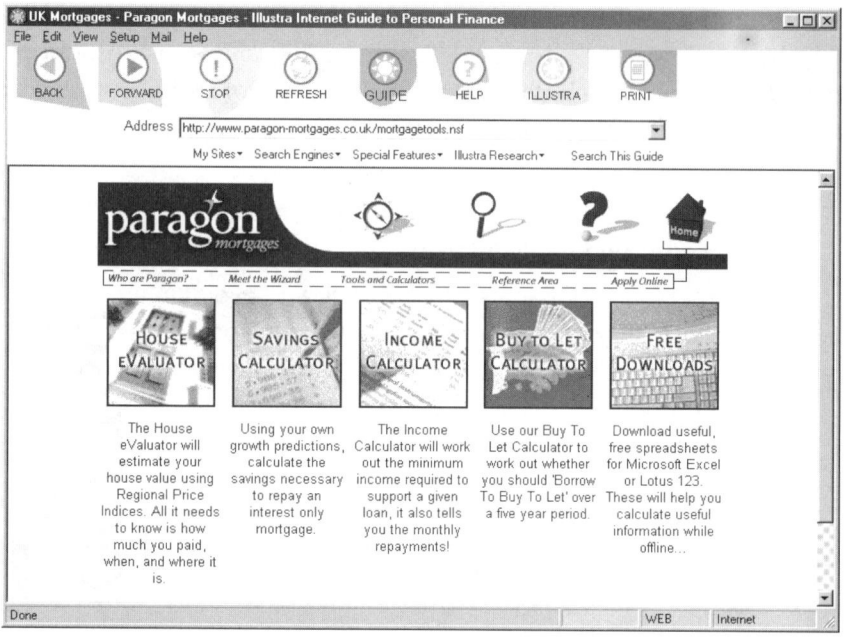

---

### Top Tip – getting online quotes

Most online quotes on offer are not instantaneous – you need to e-mail an application form, and sometimes wait up to 10 days for a response. You can sometimes fill in a form for a quick quote, but you will need to contact the lender for a more accurate figure before you make a deal.

---

The following is an illustration of the kind of comparison you can get using **Moneynet**. This site contains a database of current mortgage offers, which are revised daily. You enter the details of your existing mortgage, including redemption penalties, and it provides you with what can be a large range of alternatives. You can see from the underlined text links that some companies have Web sites or online quotations, and you can click through directly to them.

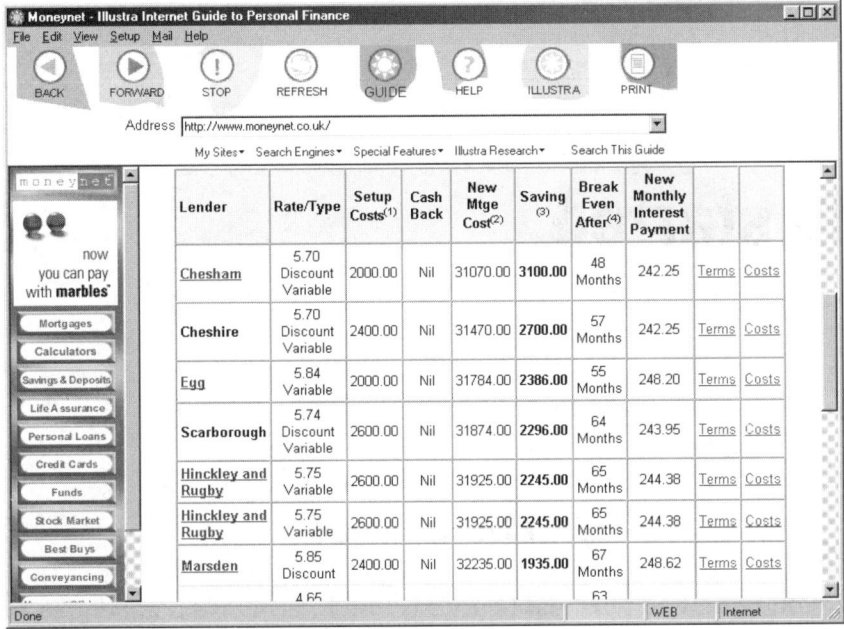

In contrast are the personal finance 'corporate brochure' sites described in Chapter 3. We've not included them in the Top 200, but they're worth a mention as you're bound to come across them on the Net. These sites offer nothing more than an online version of the company's printed brochures, so they're only useful if you want basic company information. You're probably better off visiting the 'bricks and mortar store' for more detailed and accurate information. Remember that most of the sites you'll be visiting are owned by a business whose ultimate goal is to sell you something, and some sites that purport to offer 'resources' are just 'cunningly concealed commercials'. If you're after basic information about a particular financial service, and you don't want the service provider's soft sell, go to one of the more general finance sites we've listed to get independent information and advice.

# 6

# Getting started

## The basics

If you're new to personal finance or the Internet it's a good idea to start with General personal finance – Finance basics (see page 72).

## Key points

Personal finance Web sites can offer:

- detailed information for beginners ranging from money management techniques to complex financial topics;
- tax calculators and income tax tables;
- mortgage, insurance, loan and banking comparison tables;
- yearly bills price forecasts;
- up-to-date financial news;
- stock prices.

The sites we list contain a huge amount of useful information. You may want to decide which one you prefer and use it first whenever you're online for finance matters. Most of the sites here are best described as news sites, though some may become your 'firm favourites', offering solid interactive features and useful independent advice. We've chosen a few below to highlight some of the best features you'll find.

## CASE STUDY:
## Your first stop for personal finance online

You're new to using the Internet for finance purposes, and would like to get a better grasp of what's out there.
    Click the **Blays** site in Finance basics.

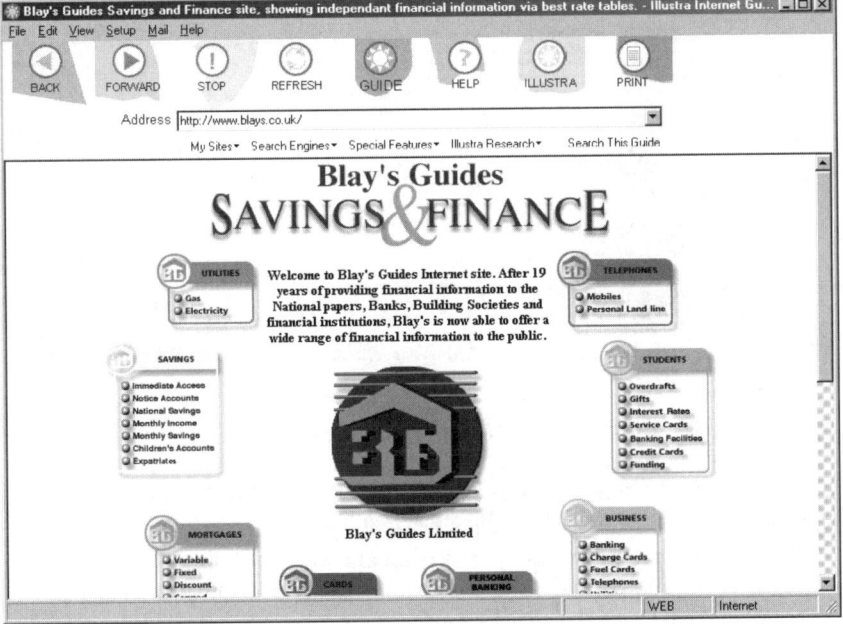

Clicking on Personal Banking and then PC Banking you find some good basic advice on PC and Internet banking. As well as a list of online banks, the site offers a gas and electricity bill calculator, which projects the cost of your utility bills.
    At the **MoneyWorld** site you'll find another, more comprehensive guide to online banking, and you can explore pages on savings and insurance. In the

insurance section, you read about getting online quotes, and note that these are given by **Screentrade**. A good frequently asked questions (FAQ) list helps settle some issues you were concerned about.

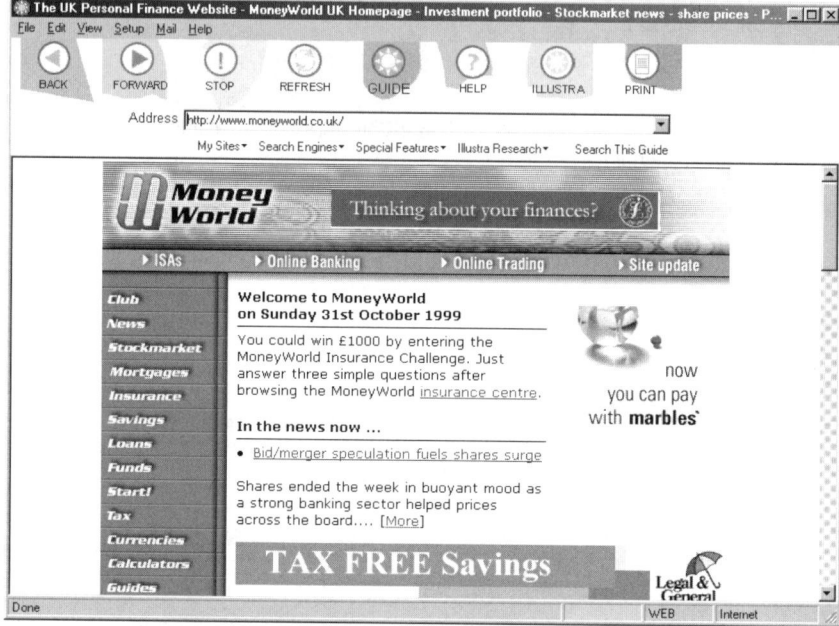

You're slightly concerned by the barrage of advertisements and wonder whether the government has any advice to offer beginners.

You try the personal finance section of the **Office of Fair Trading**. As you'd expect from the types of Web sites we've introduced in Chapter 3, this is a 'dull but worthy' site. It's heavy on text but crammed with useful information.

You have to squint to read the menu items in the left-hand column, but find that all of them lead to helpful electronic brochures.

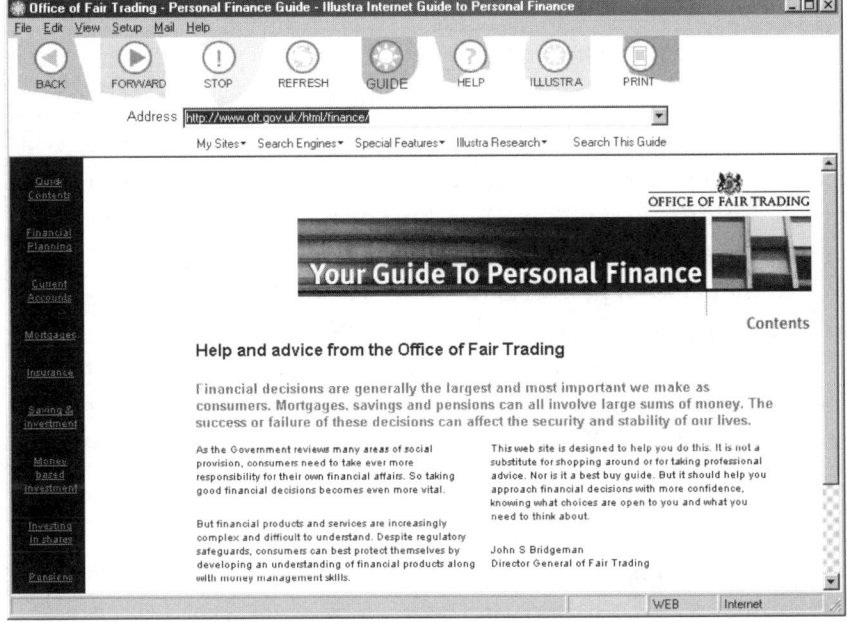

# Mortgages

## Key points

Use the Internet to find:

- basic advice and information for the beginner;

- property searches including best deals of the week;

- advice on moving;

- information on the area you're planning to move to;

- interactive features linking to the lenders most suitable to your needs;

- mortgage repayment calculators;

- estimates of the value of your home;

- loan calculators that tell you how much is needed to secure a loan, or how much you'll need to save;

- online quotes;
- online mortgage services.

Finding your own property and getting the right mortgage will involve decisions about some of the most important financial investments you're ever likely to make. Using the Internet to shop around for your mortgage will save you time and hassle. You can compare rates from a number of lenders, all on one page, rather than having to visit them individually. Some of the sites below offer the option of arranging a mortgage online, but this is still a relatively new feature. Given the complexity of most mortgage deals, you may be better off using the Web sites as a convenient method of finding out more about the rates and services on offer, thinking about the best mortgage for you, and then going to your local branch.

## CASE STUDY:
## Getting a mortgage online

You've decided you'd like to take the plunge and take out a mortgage for your first home. So where do you start? You probably know little or nothing about mortgages apart from the fact that you want one.

Here's how to use the guide to take you from the definition of a mortgage to the keys to your new home. Start by reading the guide to mortgages in the Personal Finance section of the **Office of Fair Trading** Web site. You'll find information here on the different types of mortgage rates available, repayments and fees and charges.

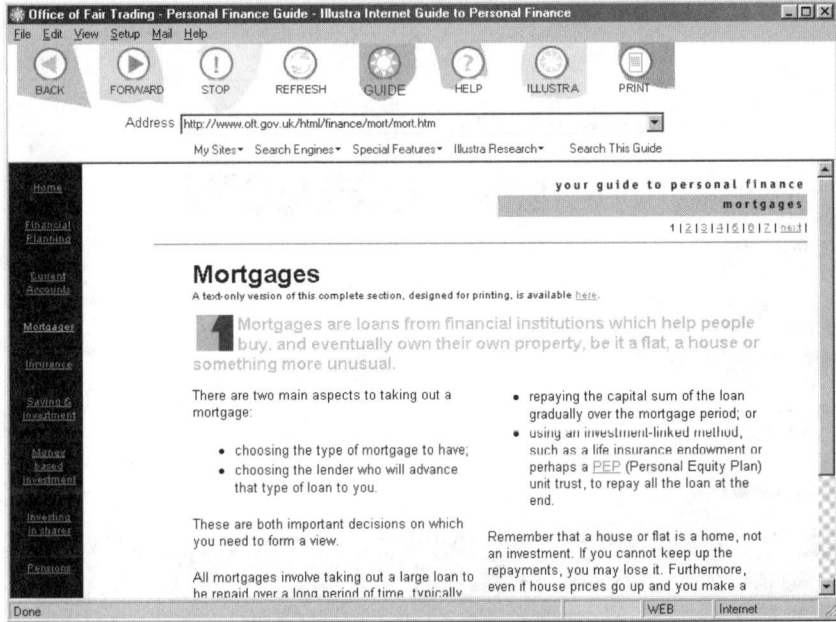

Next find an independent quote online. Try **Mortgages-Online** and click on First Time Buyer. Scroll down the text and click on Best Buys.

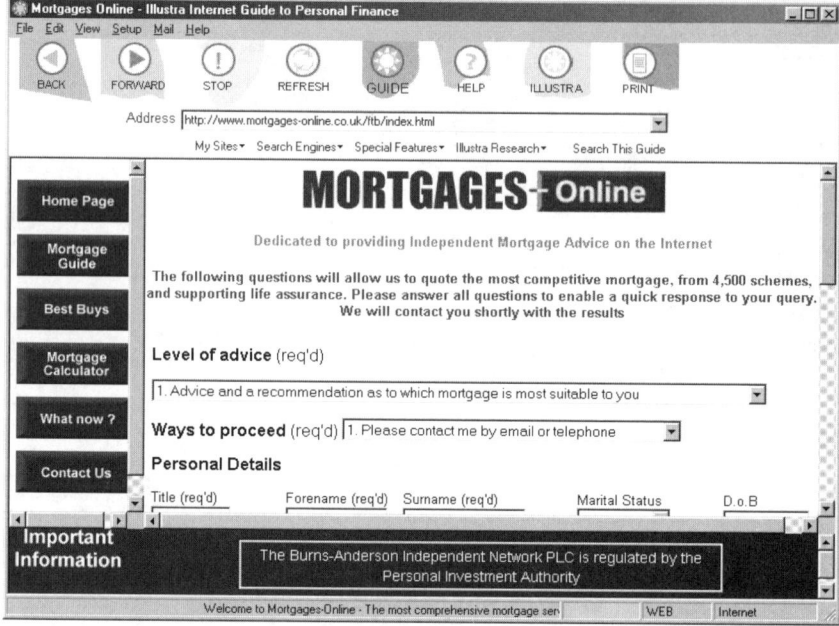

Fill in and submit the form provided and receive your quote, which will be given to you by e-mail or phone. There are other sites owned by specific mortgage providers who provide instant quotes online; you'll find these in the guide.

A mortgage calculator is useful to work out what you can afford to borrow. There are several in the guide; the following comes from the online version of **Your Mortgage** magazine. You enter the amount you want to borrow, the number of years over which you will be paying it back, and the interest rate you've been quoted.

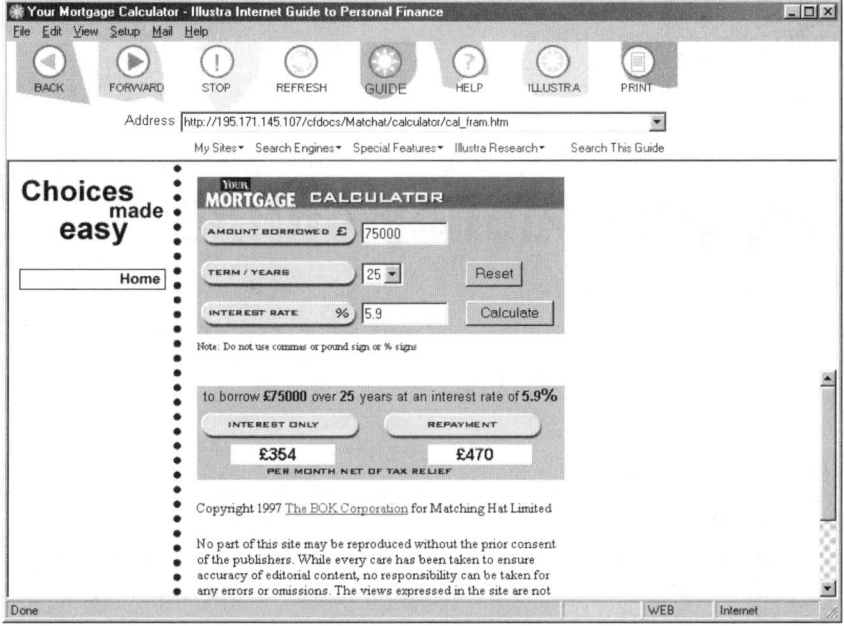

Now you know what you can afford to pay, you look for help in finding a house. There are sites that give details of properties for sale, but at the time of writing they feature few houses and are not yet a substitute for looking in estate agents' windows. But to get an idea of what online house-hunting is like, you choose the **Home Directory** site from the guide, which claims to have the largest number available. You choose SW London as your favoured area, and a maximum price of £150,000. The site returns 171 properties, and you can scroll down the list and click through to get the estate agents' phone numbers.

# 7

# Handling your money online

In this chapter we'll see how you can use *The Top 200 Web Sites for Personal Finance* to help you manage your money. You may want to try online banking, or you may just want to use the Net to get advice. We deal with banking, saving and investing, and show you how you can find banks and investment funds that operate on ethical principles.

## Banking

### Key points

On the Internet you can find:

- online banking services;
- downloadable information guides on finance matters;
- financial calculators that work out details of loans in seconds;
- the location of your nearest cash machine.

Online banking in the UK is developing and will become much more common in the next few years. High Street banks have been relatively slow to embrace the Internet, and some waited for the 'millennium bug' scare to pass before starting online services, but they are now beginning to roll out their offerings. Some banks offer online services to existing customers only, others allow you to open a new account online. Much publicity has surrounded start-up Web sites, such as **egg** and **smile**, that have used new branding to convey an up-to-date 'Net-savvy' image. Such sites claim to undercut the High Street 'bricks and mortar' banks, but you'll need to check these claims carefully.

In most cases, the High Street banks that do not yet offer online banking do have a Web site, often with useful interactive features. The guide includes a number of online sites (see Banking – Online, on pages 76–77), but if you want to keep up to date it would be a good idea to log on to the Illustra Research Web site (by clicking the Illustra button on the guide) to see if we've discovered new ones.

If you are interested in finding a home for your savings, you can use the guide to check out who offers the best rates.

---

### CASE STUDY:
### Finding the account with the highest interest rate

You have £2000 to invest and you're looking for the best rates for an instant access savings account with a cash card.

An excellent place to start is **MoneyNet**, which maintains a database of financial services. On the home page you click Savings and Deposits, then Instant Access, then Search. You key in the relevant details and press Submit. The site returns details of 45 different accounts, with a handy checklist of features. The site is updated daily to keep pace with the constant changes as new services are offered, and, of course, interest rates fluctuate in line with Bank of England base rates.

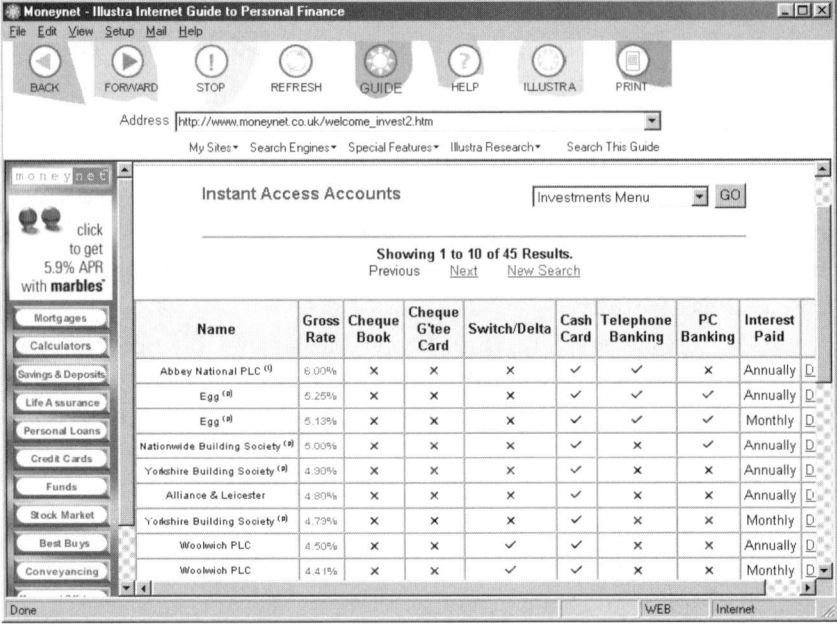

# Saving

## Key points

Using Web sites dealing with savings you can:

- invest in an ISA (individual savings account) online;
- find sites that compile the latest press articles about ISAs;
- get basic information on all aspects covering the new ISAs;
- look at comparison charts detailing where to find the most competitive rates for your ISA;
- find the best savings account for you, and work out the interest you can expect to get from it.

The plethora of different accounts from different providers can make comparisons very difficult. Complex consumer decision-making is an area in which the Internet excels, since you can easily search powerful databases to find something that meets your requirements.

## CASE STUDY:
## Finding out about ISAs online

You know that the ISA has replaced the TESSA and PEP as the government's new tax-free savings scheme. Your knowledge of the subject, however, just about ends there.

You can find some useful basic information at the **b2** site. You note that **b2** sells only its own products, and recommends you consider independent financial advice if you are not sure whether you want to buy them.

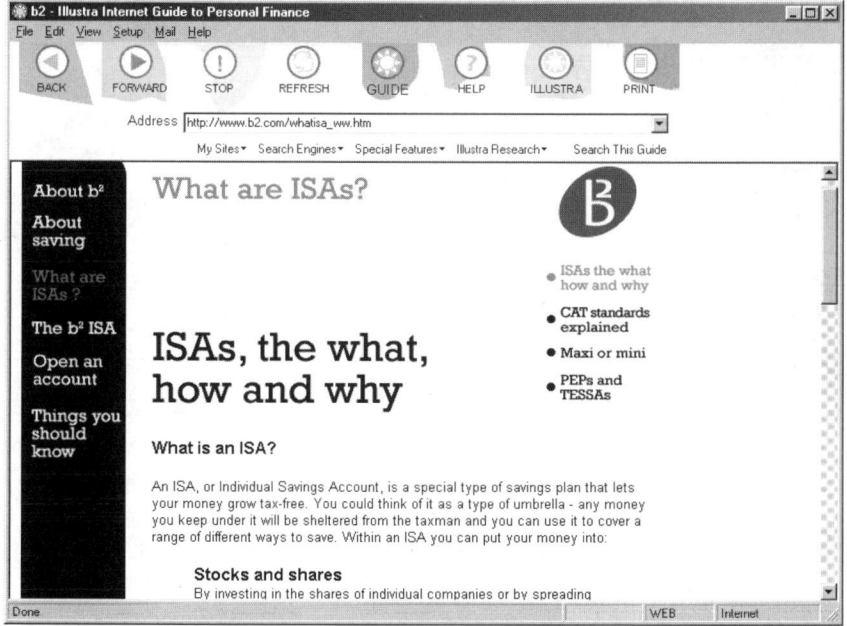

You learn the difference between a mini and maxi ISA, and the three different ways in which to invest in one or the other. Once you've decided you've got enough information about ISAs from this site, you decide to read what the press has to say before committing yourself to this new type of savings account.

At the **netISA** site you'll find articles from the national daily papers, dating back to 1997. You can find out whether leading independent financial advisers believe CAT standard ISAs are a good idea or not, for example, and there are other equally useful tips for you to consider before you take the plunge and part with your money.

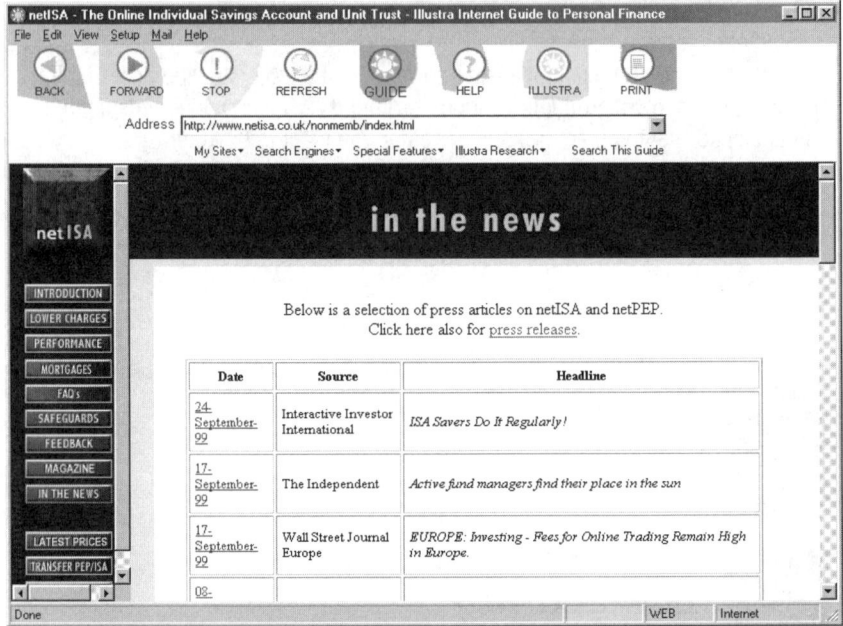

You'd probably like to compare ISA rates and see where you can get the best deal. Go to the **MoneyExtra** site, which maintains a database of different ISAs. You click on ISA and get a series of questions about the type of ISA you're looking for. Let's say, for example, you'd like to invest £120 per month into a cash ISA that allows you to give up to six months' notice of withdrawal. After entering these details you'll see a table that lists the highest-interest ISAs available specifically for this type of account. Click Contact Provider for the bank that seems to offer the best deal, and you're given their physical and Web addresses.

If you can't find the Web address of the bank you're after, check RJE's **bankweb.com** for a comprehensive listing of all UK banks and building societies.

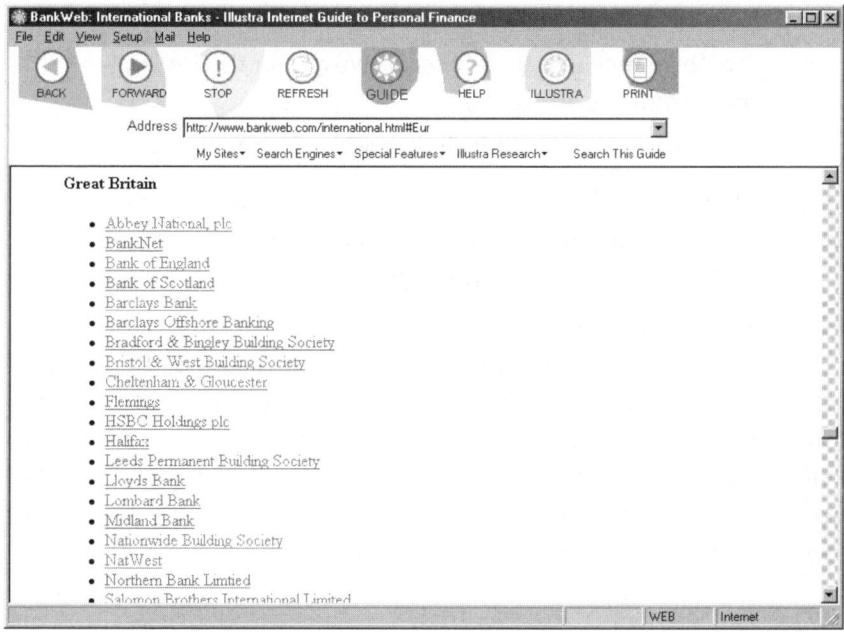

Once you've found the bank you're after, have a look at its Web site for more in-depth information on the terms and conditions of the ISA you're interested in.

# Investing

## Key points

Web sites dealing with investing can offer:

- online share dealing;
- international stock coverage;
- portfolio tracking and management facilities;
- online tutorials for the beginner;
- daily updated financial news;

- in-depth stock performance history and analysis;

- performance league tables showing you the highest-performing unit trusts;

- daily updated world indices and exchange rates;

- online financial magazines;

- advice from top brokers and access to newsgroups and forums containing useful tips and gossip about the market.

Independent investors now have access through the Internet to a vast array of information online, for which previously they would have had to pay a broker. From in-depth company reports to portfolio services offered at discounted rates, it seems now is the time to learn to invest, and to learn it online. Compared to stock market investors just a couple of years ago, you now have access to a lot more information.

## CASE STUDY:
## How to invest online

You'd like to begin investing your money in shares and, knowing that fees are lower online, you'd like to invest through an online broker. Where do you start?

Suppose you've heard rumours that a major London-based retailer is planning to expand nationwide, and that its earnings are at an all-time high. How would you find out, online, the truth in these rumours before deciding to buy shares in the company?

You could begin with **ft.com**, the online version of the *Financial Times*. Here you'll have access to up-to-date information, including the latest company and market news.

You click on Companies News and notice an article about the London retailer that confirms what you have heard – the company is expanding, and profits from its new Manchester-based branch are already exceeding expectation. You then go back to the home page and click on Company Briefs, followed by Analyst Estimates. This is where the Web site may tell you what percentage of brokers recommend to buy or sell. In this case you find that 56% recommend buying shares in the company.

Before you do, you'd like to analyse the company's performance history. You locate the **Wright Research Center** in the guide, and enter the company name into the search box.

The site will produce a five-year performance history of the company. A graph charting yearly earnings and dividends tells you that both have shown a constant increase since 1998. You're now almost certain that you'd like to buy shares but decide to have a look at the company reports before parting with your money.

You find the **CAROL** site in the guide (see Business essentials, on page 66 – or you can type CAROL in Search This Guide). You search under the alphabetical listings for the retailer and gain access to its online annual reports. Here you read the company's financial statement, including its investment plans and financial summary. You read that the company is also planning to trade online by next year, with a good profit forecast. The financial summaries and projections have confirmed your good impressions, and you decide you will indeed buy some shares.

Finally you try the **Charles Schwab** site, and click through to Europe and the UK Stock Market.

You complete the registration process and buy shares in the company you've researched. You're not expecting overnight returns, and look forward to monitoring the movement of the share price on one of the stock market news sites in the guide, such as **Interactive Investor International**.

# Ethical finance

## Key points

Using the Internet you can:

- monitor the ethical performance of major high street companies, and discover which are the most ethical;
- find an ethical independent financial adviser;
- compare rates for different ethical funds;
- investigate online banking with ethical UK banks.

Ethical investing has been around for a while, but in the 1990s it became increasingly popular. There are now over 40 ethical investment funds in the UK, making it simpler to invest ethically while still gaining competitive returns.

You can expect to find fewer ethical finance sites on the Web than ordinary investment sites. This reflects ethical funds' relatively recent status as a viable investment prospect. The sites in the guide will provide you with a good introduction to the concept of ethical investing, and link you to a number of financial institutions that offer ethical funds as well as regular banking services.

## CASE STUDY:
## Finding an ethical fund online

You're interested in investing ethically, and would like to find out how well ethical funds compare with regular funds.

Click onto **The Ethical Partnership** (see Ethical finance, on page 99) and you'll find a chart listing all UK ethical funds and their interest rate performance over a 10-year period.

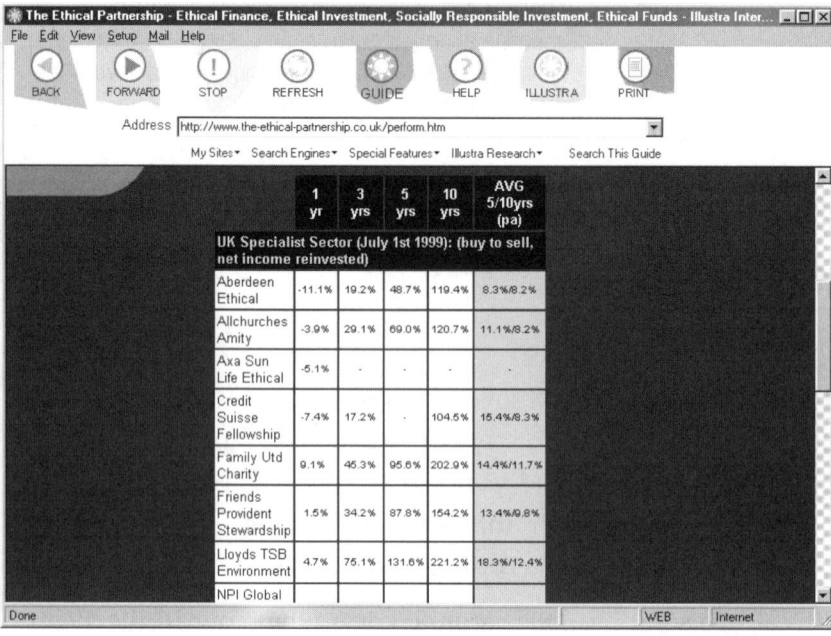

| | 1 yr | 3 yrs | 5 yrs | 10 yrs | AVG 5/10yrs (pa) |
|---|---|---|---|---|---|
| **UK Specialist Sector (July 1st 1999): (buy to sell, net income reinvested)** | | | | | |
| Aberdeen Ethical | -11.1% | 19.2% | 48.7% | 119.4% | 8.3%/8.2% |
| Allchurches Amity | -3.9% | 29.1% | 69.0% | 120.7% | 11.1%/8.2% |
| Axa Sun Life Ethical | -5.1% | . | . | . | . |
| Credit Suisse Fellowship | -7.4% | 17.2% | . | 104.5% | 15.4%/8.3% |
| Family Utd Charity | 9.1% | 45.3% | 95.6% | 202.9% | 14.4%/11.7% |
| Friends Provident Stewardship | 1.5% | 34.2% | 87.8% | 154.2% | 13.4%/9.8% |
| Lloyds TSB Environment | 4.7% | 75.1% | 131.6% | 221.2% | 18.3%/12.4% |
| NPI Global | | | | | |

This shows which ethical fund is the highest performer. You may want to find out how the fund has gained its ethical status. Either go to the fund's Web site, or try the **UK Social Investment Forum**. If you click on Members you get a list of UK banks and building societies who are recognized as members of the UK Social Investment Forum. You can then get details of how the banks on the list are performing and investing ethically.

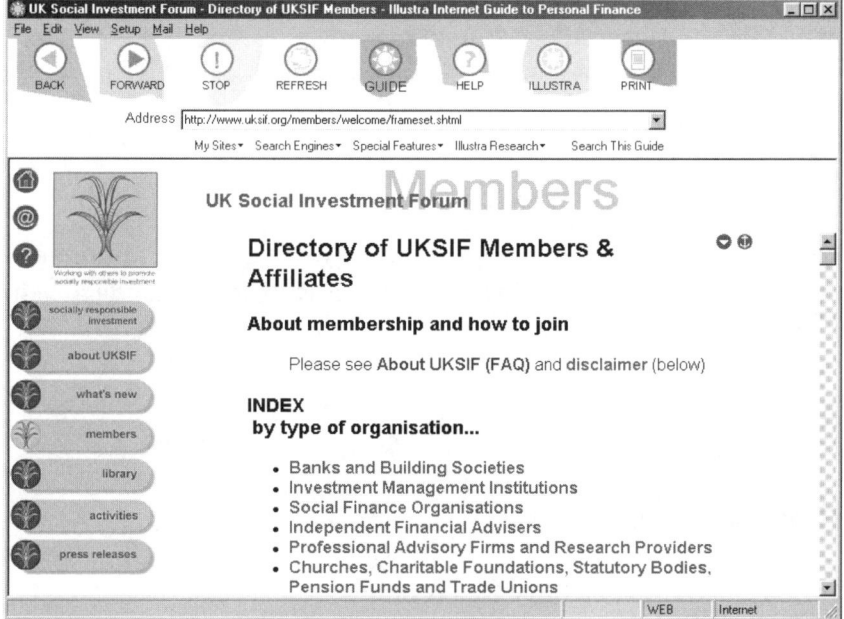

# 8

# Paying out – tax and insurance

Personal finance is about paying out as well as saving and investments, and in this chapter we show you how to use the guide to help you with tax and insurance.

## Tax

### Key points

Various Web sites dealing with tax offer:

- relevant tax forms to download;
- tips on filling out self-assessment forms;
- information about the latest Budget;
- essential information on all tax matters.

Tax is one of the less inspiring, but unfortunately essential, aspects of personal finance, and it is also making an appearance on the Web. Perhaps unsurprisingly, we haven't found many enthralling or truly original sites covering tax, though there is much useful information to be had. You'll find that tax sites are either produced by the government or independent tax advisory firms, and in most cases they've yet to take full advantage of what the Internet can do. Nonetheless, these sites are worth a visit for the essential information they offer. We have not tried to compile lists of independent financial advisers or accountants, but where possible have found sites that help you to find the right kind of professional advice.

## CASE STUDY:
## Finding out about self-assessment

You've struggled by somehow with the new system of self-assessment, but now you feel it's time to get a better grip just in case you've been paying too much tax.

The logical place to start is the **Inland Revenue** site, one of the 'dull but worthy' sites we described in Chapter 3. Click on Self-assessment and then choose the graphics version, where you will find some simple-to-follow information. You will also be able to download self-assessment and tax returns forms here.

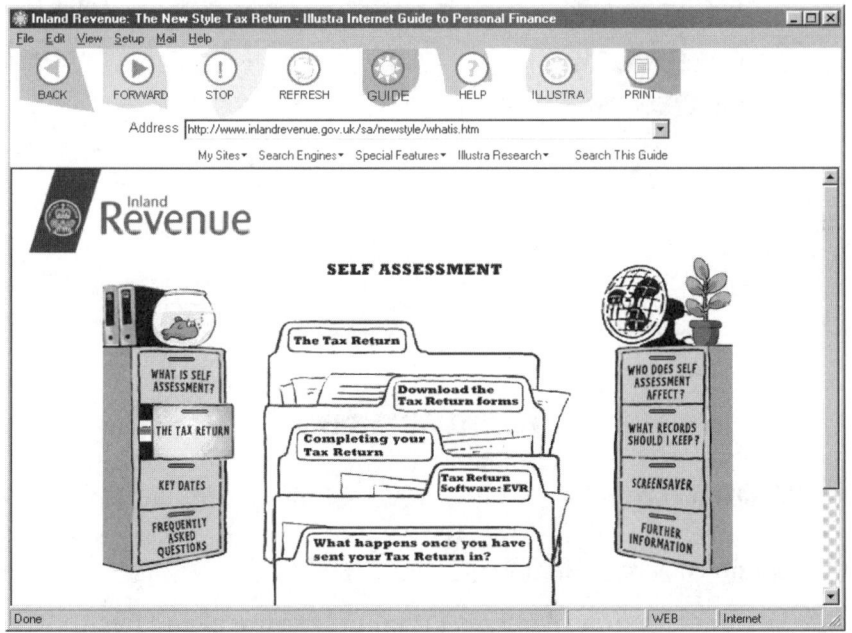

If you go back to the home page and click on Individuals Guide you will find the Self-assessment Guide, which takes you through the myriad steps in filling out your newly downloaded self-assessment form. If you prefer, you can download a piece of software called EVR that will prompt you as you fill in the form on your PC. You can then sign it and send it in to your tax office.

The site from **Line One** has plenty of advice and tips and some useful tools including a tax calculator. It's less dull but no less worthy than the **Inland Revenue** site, and it makes it a bit less tedious to work through your tax position. You can also keep up to date with the latest tax rates here, with the PricewaterhouseCooper's tax-rate tables.

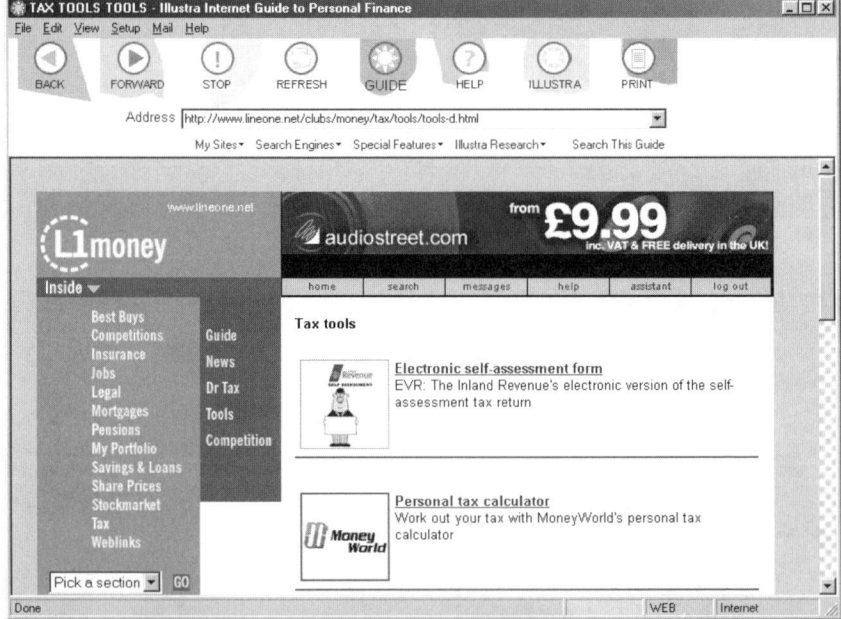

# Insurance

## Key points

On the Internet you will find:

■ online insurance quotes for home, car, travel and health;

- comparison charts for UK-wide insurance policies, leading you to the best deals around;
- insurance calculators that help you assess how much you can afford to pay;
- sites that will sell you insurance online;
- downloadable consumer guides.

Most insurance Web sites are 'corporate brochures', and we have not included them in this guide unless they offer something apart from promoting their own products. The ones we've chosen will at the very least offer some interactive features, such as online quotes and insurance calculators, while some of the more advanced ones offer the option to purchase online. Look out for deals to be made while purchasing online – some insurance companies are offering up to 20 per cent discounts for online purchases.

## CASE STUDY:
## Finding the right insurance policy online

You think it's time to review your home insurance, but don't know how much your property is worth.

The **Legal & General** site has some smart features that you will find helpful in assessing your insurance needs. Click on Home Insurance, then Home Contents, then Interactive Home.

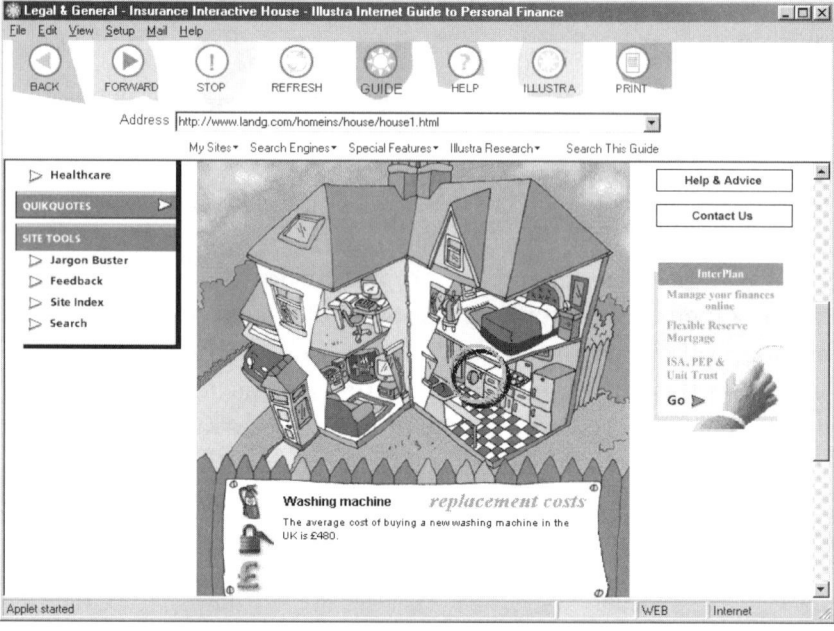

The house is a cleverly designed tool, which gives you relevant advice on your home security, fire prevention and replacement costs. Roll your mouse over the house to get a good idea of how much your main household items would cost to replace if stolen or damaged. If you weren't convinced you needed contents insurance before, you will be after looking at the starting costs of some of these appliances.

To get some online quotes, try **Screentrade.** Click on Home Insurance and you'll find a long form asking you to provide details of the type of home insurance you require. Fill this out and you'll receive cost comparisons of home insurance policies that suit your needs. You can then decide whether to visit the site of the insurance company offering the best rates, or even purchase your insurance cover online.

**Direct Line** is another company who gives online quotes and the opportunity to buy a policy online. The online quotation tool takes a while to download, but the response is quick once you've entered the details on the form. If you're happy with their offer, you have the option to click on Buy Online and receive a discount, or to save the quote and amend your details.

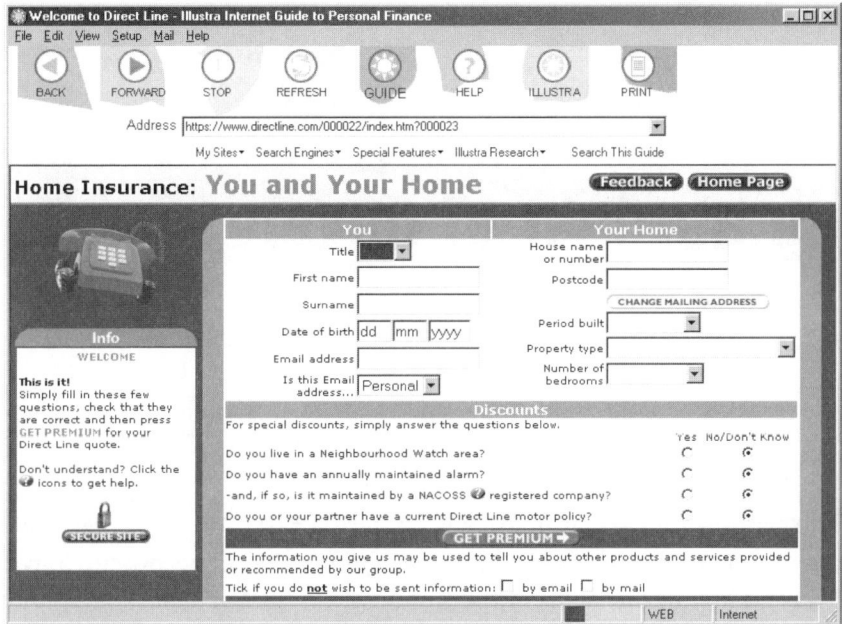

# 9

# Keeping abreast of developments

The world of personal finance is changing fast, not just because of the impact of the Internet. Consumer bodies and governments have been taking an interest in how financial services are marketed, and have been concerned with the small print of mortgages and insurance policies.

You can use the guide to keep yourself informed of developments. If you catch the investing bug, for example, you can subscribe to online newsletters and take part in discussion forums where other investors talk about their experiences.

You will also want to search the Internet for material not included in the guide. The final section of this chapter gives you some tips on doing this.

## Financial news

### Key points

Look on financial news Web sites for:

- access to the trading strategies and top tips of some of the most respected global strategists;

- in-depth information and analysis that would be difficult or expensive to obtain from print publications;
- general financial news online;
- a searchable archive of past news articles and topics;
- a daily round-up of finance headlines throughout the world.

Many online newsletters and magazines are available on a sub-scription basis only, so if you are looking at material on a Web site and you haven't subscribed, the chances are you are reading infor-mation that is either abridged or out of date. Always make sure of what you're reading before you trust the information. Having said that, you can get valuable information free on the Internet (at least for the time being) and the sites we've chosen for the Top 200 do offer a substantial amount of material. You'll find financial and business news updated to the last 5 minutes in the **NewsNow** service and daily market analysis with 20-minute-delayed share prices.

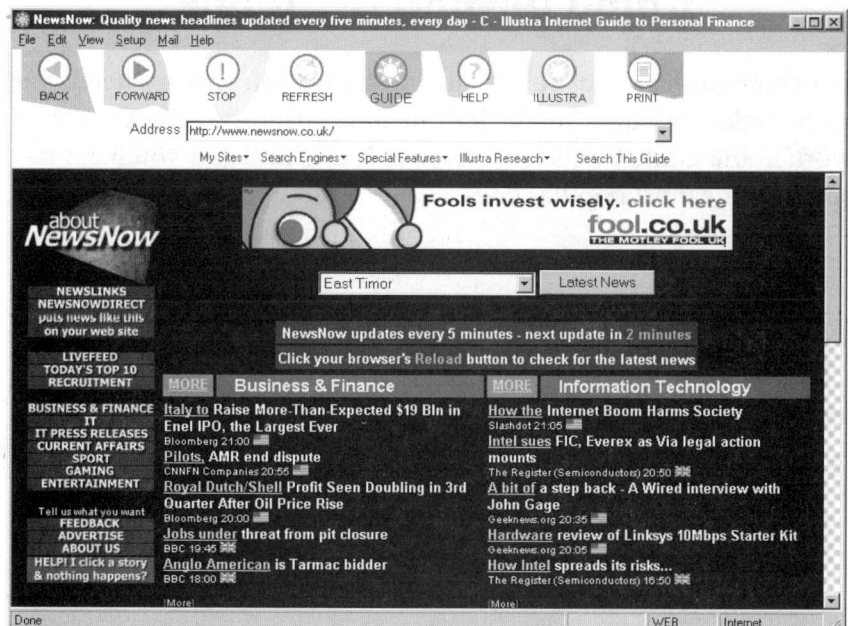

Some sites offer an e-mail newsletter service, in which subscribers are automatically sent a regular digest to their inbox. This saves the trouble of logging on to the site each day to receive the latest news. Subscribe to the newsletter services you find the most useful, remembering it's as well to be selective – it's very easy to oversubscribe and find your inbox full of information that you will never get around to reading. E-mail services from good sites will offer clear instructions somewhere in the text of each message explaining how to remove yourself (or 'unsubscribe') from the list.

When you register or give your e-mail address to subscribe to services, many sites offer you an option to allow them to contact you about other services. Sometimes, this option is automatically selected unless you specifically 'un-check' the box on the registration form. Be careful of exposing yourself to regular unsolicited or junk e-mail. The best policy in these cases is to carefully check the contents of the electronic form you are submitting.

# Going beyond the guide

Search engines are not easy to use, and they often overwhelm you with irrelevant sites. You'll find an introduction to the way they work in the guide by clicking on Search Engines, and you'll get fast access to the most popular ones.

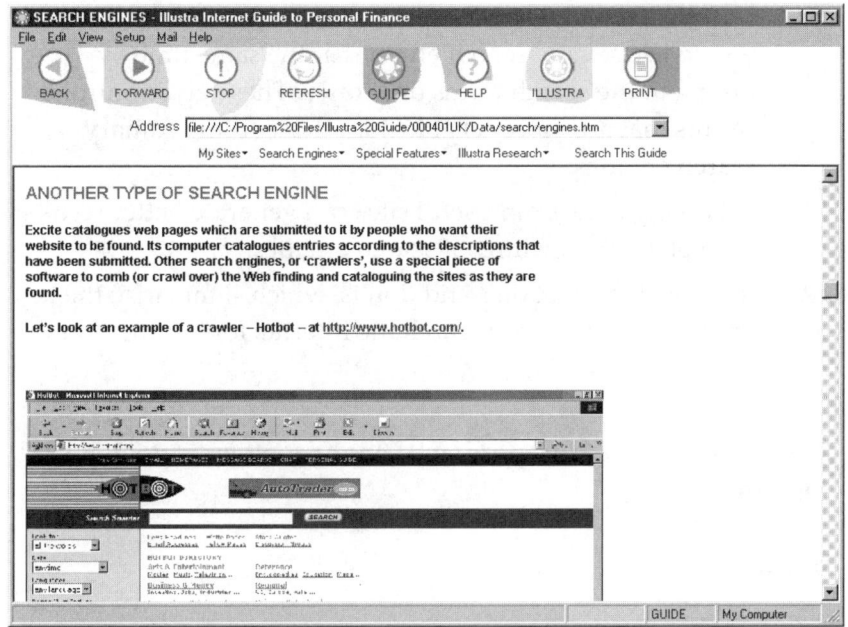

# How to maximize your search successes

You need to be prepared and focused on what you are looking for when you search the Web. Many users experience frustration using the Web because they can't find the information they require. This frustration is not only created by the low quality of much of what's available, but because these users haven't clearly thought through what sort of information they require. The more focused you are in what types of sites you are looking for, the more successful you are likely to be.

# Searching hints

▓ When you first reach a Web site check for a physical address and/or a date so that you can eliminate irrelevant US sites or those that are out of date or abandoned.

■ Use meta search engines such as Copernic, which allow you to use several search engines at the same time by typing in the search terms only once. These give controlled results that are more reliable than those from ordinary search engines.

■ Following links from useful sites can generate better results than blanket 'trawling' of search engines.

And finally, here is a list of do's and don'ts, which summarize the key points to remember when you search the Internet for information.

---

**WWW searching for personal finance sites – do's and don'ts**

**Do…**

Work out what type of information you want before you start.

Use Web sites types to help you decide what sites you've reached and what sites you are looking for. If the sites you have found don't tally with what you want to find, then leave quickly.

Use more specific search terms because they will get you better results.

Put 'UK' in your search terms because it will help you eliminate US sites, which are less likely to be useful to British users.

Check the date of the last update when you find a site, since this will save time wasted on redundant or abandoned sites.

**Don't…**

Feel that you should 'plough' through all search results you

---

return because this will inevitably waste time. Doing this is like feeling that you have to read every detail in a newspaper. Instead, make sure that you read selectively.

Key in 'personal finance uk' as a search string and then wonder why you can't find out what you want.

Search at peak times unless you want the Web to 'plod along' at a frustratingly slow pace. The best time to search is between 4 am and 7 am when the Web is wonderfully fast because the US market is asleep and not online.

*Good luck!*

# The Top 200 Web sites for personal finance

| Sub Topic | Title | Description | URL | Rele-vance | Ease of Use |
|-----------|-------|-------------|-----|-----------|-------------|
| **BUSINESS ESSENTIALS** | | | | | |
| *BUSINESS INFORMATION* | | The following sites contain financial, company and product information of value to any business user. | | | |
| | Interactive Investor International | Instant stock market quotes and access to some (occasionally) lively discussions from shareholders. Registration required. | www.iii.co.uk/ | 1 | 3 |
| | Yahoo! Finance UK & Ireland | Simple instant stock market quotes without registration. | finance.uk. yahoo.com/ | 1 | 4 |
| | CAROL | A set of over 3000 company reports from large companies in the UK, Asia and Europe. Registration is free to companies, but coverage can be patchy. You are transferred to the company's Web site, so reports are not in a standard format. | www.carol.co.uk/ | 1 | 2 |
| | Companies House | Model Web site, beautifully designed. You can search the database for company information but (strangely) only on Monday to Friday from 8 am to 8 pm. | www.companies-house.gov.uk | 2 | 3 |

| Sub Topic | Title | Description | URL | Rele-vance | Ease of Use |
|---|---|---|---|---|---|
| | How many online? | NUA Internet surveys collect data from around the world and give you the latest picture of how many people have Internet access in different countries. | www.nua.ie/surveys /how_many_online /index.html | 1 | 2 |
| | UpMyStreet | Enter your postcode and find out what your neighbourhood's really like. Gives data on house prices, crime clear-up rates, schools, council tax, and, if you're feeling fragile, ambulance response times. More features promised soon. | www.upmystreet.com/ | 2 | 4 |
| | Scoot | One of the most useful and friendly sites around. Search by business type and area for anything you need. Free registration is required to use the people finder, which claims 17 million names on its database. | www.scoot.co.uk/ | 4 | 5 |
| *TRAVEL* | | Getting about is so much easier with this kind of constantly updated information at your fingertips. These sites provide a good excuse for spending money on a mobile Web terminal. | | | |
| | A2B Travel | A bit cluttered and not fully comprehensive, but this is the best general UK travel site we've encountered. | www.a2btravel.com/ | 3 | 2 |
| | Expedia UK | Microsoft's UK travel site is an essential asset for the business traveller, but don't expect bargain travel here. It's simple to find scheduled flights, hotels and car hire in major cities and compare prices before you book. | expedia.co.uk/ | 3 | 4 |
| | UK Public Transport Information | The site says 'If it's not here, it's not on the Web' and for once it's not hype. Everything you need to know about public transport in any part of the UK. | www.pti.org.uk/ | 4 | 4 |

| Sub Topic | Title | Description | URL | Rele-vance | Ease of Use |
|---|---|---|---|---|---|
| | Railtrack | If you simply want train times Railtrack's online timetable is the quickest way to get them. | 195.92.21.203/bin/ query.exe/en | 4 | 3 |
| | BAA Airport Information | Updates arrivals for major UK airports, and shows a flight timetable. You can also find out what's in the shops to buy while you're waiting for the flight. | www.baa.co.uk/ | 4 | 4 |
| | World maps | Not just any old maps but just about every kind of map that might be out there. Some are detailed enough to see the street you're headed for, but most provide political, economic or geographical information that may be useful if you don't know a country well. | www.lib.utexas.edu/ Libs/PCL/Map_ collection/Map_ collection.html | 1 | 1 |
| | OANDA Currency Converter | How many Albanian lek to the euro? No problem with this comprehensive and simple currency converter. You can also find historical rates for any day since 1990. | www.oanda.com/ converter/classic | 3 | 4 |
| | Multimap.com | A clickable map, down to street level, of the whole UK. Or simply enter a place name, or postcode, and get a map that you can zoom in and out of. Terrific! | uk.multimap.com/ map/places.cgi | 4 | 5 |
| *WEATHER AND TIME* | | Time to find out whether you need an umbrella. | | | |
| | The Met. Office | The weather – 'straight from the horse's mouth'. | www.meto.govt.uk/ | 1 | 4 |
| | The World Clock | Is it too late to call Melbourne? Instant time anywhere in the world. | www.timeanddate. com/worldclock/ | 2 | 1 |
| *TELEPHONE AND POST* | | Essentials about essentials. | | | |
| | Postcodes On-line | Find addresses from postcodes and vice versa. | www.royalmail.co.uk/ paf/pcodefin.htm | 4 | 4 |

| Sub Topic | Title | Description | URL | Rele-vance | Ease of Use |
|-----------|-------|-------------|-----|-----------|-------------|
| | UK Telephone code locator | In which part of the country is that number beginning 01736? (Penzance, actually). What's the code for Penrith? A simple and handy tool developed by an enthusiast. | www.warwick.ac.uk/cgi-bin-Phones/nng | 2 | 1 |
| | BT PhoneNet UK | The UK phone book online. Even if you pay a dial-up call, it's cheaper than dialling 192. | www.bt.com/phonenetuk/ | 4 | 4 |
| | BT Friends and Family | Change your friends and family numbers at a stroke. You can also check the current status of your phone bill. | https://www.customer-service.bt.com/friends_family/owa/bestfriend.who | 2 | 2 |
| *NEWS AND MEDIA* | | The best sites we've found for information about television, radio, newspapers and magazines | | | |
| | BBC News | The front page of the BBC's news Web site. You can link directly to the last news bulletin on the World Service or on BBC1, if your browser's equipped for sound and video. | news.bbc.co.uk/ | 2 | 4 |
| | AskMagpie | Links to over 7000 magazines and often very specialist journals organized by subject in a well-laid-out front page. Sounds daunting, but a simple search engine allows title and subject searches. Many have Web links, but if not there are fax and phone numbers. | www.askmagpie.com/ | 3 | 4 |
| | Media UK Internet Directory | A really comprehensive index to media resources. The use of sound quickly becomes irritating, but you'll need to turn it back up for the live TV and radio. Aims to please all, but would benefit by organizing the resources according to who the user is. | www.mediauk.com/directory/ | 3 | 3 |
| | World Newspapers Online | Lovely interface with clickable map to reach 120+ English-language newspapers across the world. | www.alumni.adweb.co.uk/wno/ | 1 | 3 |

| Sub Topic | Title | Description | URL | Rele-vance | Ease of Use |
|---|---|---|---|---|---|
| | Teletext | Millions of people regularly use this service on their TV. On your computer it looks much better and is much easier to use. | www1.teletext.co.uk/ | 2 | 1 |
| | TVPlus | Quick and simple guide to what is on the five terrestrial TV channels in your region, plus a few satellite channels in peak time only. | www1.teletext.co.uk/ tv_new/ | 1 | 1 |
| *WRITING AIDS* | | The online aids can be really useful for report writing – especially if you have a permanent connection to the Internet. | | | |
| | thesaurus.com | A simple online *Roget's Thesaurus*. You can put in UK spellings but will be given US spellings. | www.thesaurus.com/ | 1 | 2 |
| | dictionary.com | Simple online dictionary based on Webster's. | www.dictionary.com/ | 1 | 2 |
| | OneLook Dictionaries | If you're really stuck or a true word lover you'll get hooked on this database, which claims to look at 2.8 million words in 566 dictionaries. | www.onelook.com/ | 1 | 2 |
| | Webopedia | Look up what all that computer jargon means. If you really want to impress in 'techie' circles click on the recently added items and add them to your 'geekspeak'. | webopedia.internet .com/ | 2 | 3 |
| | Whatis?com | Much more than a technical dictionary, this site has exploration sections on various topics, including how the Internet works, and speeds of connection. Try the learning paths section for excellent essay on technology-related topics such as 'convergence'. | www.whatis.com/ | 2 | 4 |
| | infoplease.com | A huge US-based site with a huge number of … facts! | www.infoplease.com/ | 1 | 2 |

| Sub Topic | Title | Description | URL | Rele-vance | Ease of Use |
|---|---|---|---|---|---|
| | Microsoft Encarta | Microsoft's cut-down free online version of Encarta might find out what you need, if you can bear the hard sell for the subscription version. | www.encarta.msn.com | 1 | 2 |
| *LAW AND MONEY* | | General resources – often enough to tell you whether you need to pay for professional advice. | | | |
| | adviceguide | A service from the Citizens Advice Bureau – well designed and easy to use. | www.adviceguide.org. uk/nacab/plsql/ nacab.homepage | 1 | 3 |
| | buy.co.uk | A simple but hugely effective idea. Put in your postcode and latest bill and you can see whether you'll save money by switching electricity or gas suppliers. Compares mobile phone tariffs as well. | www.buy.co.uk/ | 3 | 4 |
| *FOR ADVANCED USERS* | | These are free resources for those seriously into the Internet, or who work all day on a keyboard. | | | |
| | EBoz! | Links and tips for anyone involved in building or running a Web site, or who'd like to. Expert advice, case studies and discussion forums, and plenty of free downloads to get you going. | www.eboz.com/index. shtml | 1 | 4 |
| | AnyDay.com | If you use an electronic organizer or a program such as Microsoft Outlook you'll find this a terrific idea. You can store your information confidentially and free of charge on this site. You can synchronize it with your own data so that others (your secretary or work colleagues) can see your schedule if you share a password and log-in. | www.anyday.com/ | 2 | 4 |

| Sub Topic | Title | Description | URL | Rele-vance | Ease of Use |
|---|---|---|---|---|---|
| | Calendars Net | The site allows you to maintain calendars of events that are of interest to a group of people, free of charge. A link to Egroups (also in this section) lets you e-mail the group when new events are posted. Messy to look at, but a clever site from a public interest group in the US dedicated to improving communications and reducing global warming. | www.calendars.net/ | 3 | 2 |
| | FreeDrive | FreeDrive gives you 20 Mb of free storage space so you can get access to your files from any Web terminal when away from your desk. Your data is password protected, but you'll have to pay $4.95 a month if you want secure encryption. | www.freedrive.com/ | 1 | 3 |
| | e.groups | A cracking example of free services on the Internet. This one lets you maintain an e-mail list and bulletin board – really useful if you're working with distant colleagues or have a lot of relatives on e-mail. There's also a private chat room available if you're into that kind of thing. | www.egroups.com | 2 | 4 |

**GENERAL PERSONAL FINANCE**

| Sub Topic | Title | Description | URL | Rele-vance | Ease of Use |
|---|---|---|---|---|---|
| *FINANCE BASICS* | | Many of these sites offer you the type of financial information it would take days to compile independently. | | | |
| | Wise Money | If you have the patience to fill out the extensive free registration form, this site offers useful free quotes on insurance, loans and mortgage rates. An independent Internet financial services marketing organization, the site receives funding from advertisements placed on the site. | www.wisemoney. com/homepage.asp | 3 | 2 |

| Sub Topic | Title | Description | URL | Rele-vance | Ease of Use |
|---|---|---|---|---|---|
| | EMUnet | This non-profit site financed by sponsorship collects in one place an impressive range of unbiased information on European monetary issues. | www.euro-emu.co.uk/ | 2 | 2 |
| | Economy Web | This is an average all-rounder that basically links you to information on other Web sites. You can access UK and international company profiles, check up on 20-minute-delayed stock updates, and link to national and business publications and magazincs. | www.economyweb.com/uk.htm | 1 | 1 |
| | Money World | Offering everything from income tax tables and tax calculators to tools that calculate the best mortgage/insurance rates on offer. You can also join its online investment club for free. | www.moneyworld.co.uk/ | 2 | 2 |
| | Blays | A very comprehensive beginner's guide to the ins and outs of personal finance. Blays is a financial information service that previously dealt only with national papers and financial institutions. The company has now gone public and, judging from this site, has much to offer. Forecast your yearly electricity bill or find the highest-performing current accounts and more, all in a very user-friendly site. | www.blays.co.uk/3 | 4 | 4 |
| | Financial Planning Horizons | Offers unbiased information on most aspects of finance, including an in-depth lesson in comparing financial products from different service providers. Essential stuff for the beginner. | www.financial-planning.uk.com/ | 3 | 1 |

| Sub Topic | Title | Description | URL | Rele-vance | Ease of Use |
|---|---|---|---|---|---|
| | Times-Money | *The Times* newspaper produces this comprehensive financial guide offering advice and basic information on mortgages, pensions, tax, travel insurance, shares and more. You'll need to register for most of the stock market information, but non-subscribers do have access to 20-minute-delayed stock prices. Also includes an A–Z glossary of financial terms, and a useful comparison table of various UK savings accounts. | www.times-money. co.uk/ | 4 | 2 |
| | Chartered Insurance Institute | You can expect to find general, impartial advice from this independent charity. Offers a useful 'how to manage your money' factsheet for the absolute novice. You can buy texts dealing with financial matters online. | www.cii.co.uk/fact1.htm | 1 | 1 |
| | World microcap.com | Site for investors interested in start-ups and firms with small market capitalization. Provided by the print publication *Financial Sentinel*, who offer three free issues. Still developing at the time of review, but it promises to become a major source for small CAP investors. | www.worldmicrocap .com/ | 1 | 1 |
| | Money Web | A good solid site that is mostly text-based, making it quick and easy to read or print out. Offers useful interactive tools such as pension calculators, including a state pension projector. | www.moneyweb.co.uk | 2 | 1 |
| | Office of Fair Trading | Offers a good detailed beginners' guide to personal finance, complete with a glossary. The home page leads to information about consumer rights, such as credit and debt advice and | www.oft.gov.uk/ html/finance/ | 2 | 1 |

| Sub Topic | Title | Description | URL | Rele-vance | Ease of Use |
|---|---|---|---|---|---|
| | | how to deal with complaints. A respectable site, though not updated as often as it should be. | | | |
| | FT Quicken | The finance site from the *Financial Times*. Its slightly cumbersome layout hides some very useful material. You can find the best mortgage rates and calculate how much tax you'll be paying next year. You'll also find the day's top finance news from the FT. | www.ftquicken.co.uk/ | 3 | 1 |
| | Find | The Financial Information Net Directory provides a really comprehensive list of links for all UK finance-related topics. | www.find.co.uk/ | 3 | 3 |
| | Finance Wise | You don't have to register to use this search engine designed to find financial topics, but if you don't you'll get sick of the reminders. Unlike most search engines, the site uses human editors to index and appraise the information. You can search for companies, sectors, books and jobs. | www.financewise.com/ | 3 | 4 |
| | Money Extra | Offers a very useful service comparing ISAs, mortgages, current accounts, loans, credit cards and more. Make this a first stop before buying any UK financial products. | www.moneyextra. com/main.asp | 4 | 2 |
| | This is Money | Updated daily, this site from the *Daily Mail* and *Evening Standard* keeps track of the best mortgage deals, highest-performing unit trusts, and offers sound financial advice across the board. A jargon-free glossary and up-to-date financial news articles and calculators make this site a good and easy-to-use general personal finance resource. | www.thisismoney.com/ | 3 | 3 |

| Sub Topic | Title | Description | URL | Rele-vance | Ease of Use |
|---|---|---|---|---|---|
| **BANKING** | | | | | |
| *BANKING BASICS* | | Here you'll find some useful and sometimes even interesting information about banks in the UK. | | | |
| | Bank of England | All you ever wanted to know about the Bank of England. Includes full copies of all its published reports. | www.bankofengland.co.uk | 2 | 1 |
| | British Bankers Association | Especially useful for beginners, with a straightforward FAQ page, which includes interesting information about banks, the euro, and a 'how to do Internet banking' section. | www.bankfacts.org.uk | 1 | 1 |
| | Bank Web | A library of links to bank sites across the globe. | bankweb.com | 2 | 1 |
| *ONLINE BANKING* | | In some cases you can complete everything to set up your account online, in others you have to visit a branch to sign the paperwork. | | | |
| | egg | Enormously successful offshoot of the Prudential. This slick site showcases their savings accounts, mortgages and credit card and contains a series of downloadable guides on a variety of money matters. | www.egg.com/ | 2 | 3 |
| | smile | A new online banking service from the Co-operative Bank. Offers a full range of current and savings accounts, credit cards and an ISA in a straightforward and easy-to-use site. | www.smile.co.uk/ | 3 | 3 |
| | Allied Irish | Offering online banking and the usual interactive features on its site. Also offers a euro calculator but annoyingly this needs downloading before you can use it. Strangely you have to visit a branch to register and open an online account. | www.aib.ie/global/ | 1 | 1 |

| Sub Topic | Title | Description | URL | Rele- vance | Ease of Use |
|---|---|---|---|---|---|
| | First-Direct | First Direct were the pioneers of telephone banking in the UK, but have not yet embraced Internet banking, despite offering free Internet access. This site gives a demonstration of their PC banking service, which requires you to download their access software and install it on your PC. | www.firstdirect.co.uk/ PCBanking/html/ Index.html | 2 | 2 |
| | Royal Bank of Scotland | You can download an application form for Internet banking from this site, but you can't open an account online. Q&A feature gives you basic information, with screenshots of the different features. | www.royalbankscot. co.uk/pc&online/ default.htm | 1 | 1 |
| | NatWest | Better on travel and personal finance information than banking. At the time of review you had to pay extra for the PC banking service, and you can't set up an account online. | www.natwest.co.uk/ | 1 | 1 |
| | Halifax online | The only thing you can do without registering is view a demo of their Internet banking service, which at the time of review was for current accounts only. | www.halifax-online. co.uk/ | 1 | 1 |
| | Barclays Online Banking | A full range of banking services is available online on this helpful and easy-to-use site. Also offers free Internet access. | www.barclays.co.uk/ online.html | 3 | 3 |
| | Lloyds TSB | Online banking for those who already have Lloyds or TSB accounts. If you have one, you can apply online for Internet access to your existing account. If you haven't and you still want an account, you'll have to visit a branch. | www.lloydstsb.co.uk | 1 | 2 |

| Sub Topic | Title | Description | URL | Rele-vance | Ease of Use |
|---|---|---|---|---|---|
| *BANKS AND BLDG SOCS* | | Many of these are 'corporate brochures', but the better ones offer useful information and features. | | | |
| | Legal & General | You'll find the usual mortgage and loan repayment calculators here, with a few interesting additions such as advice on the costs of moving house. A simple and informative site. | www.landg.com | 2 | 2 |
| | Abbey National plc | Straightforward flat design, with useful mortgage rate and loan calculator. No online services, and a distinctly 'corporate brochure' feel. | www.abbeynational.co.uk | 1 | 1 |
| | Bristol & West | Basic loan and mortgage calculators including one that allows you to calculate how much you can afford to borrow. | www.bristol-west.co.uk | 1 | 1 |
| | Cheltenham & Gloucester | A well-designed site that is easy to use and informative. Offers a 'Decision in Principle' for mortgages: fill out the form and they'll send you an answer on a potential mortgage (after the information you supply is verified). You can open an investment account by downloading a form and mailing in. | www.cheltglos.co.uk/ | 2 | 2 |
| | Northern Rock | A good mortgage section where you can calculate how much you could borrow based on annual income, plus a mortgage calculator, a mortgage comparison table, and useful information for first-time buyers. Good information for beginners. | www.northernrock.co.uk | 2 | 2 |
| | HSBC | Very basic site, which offers little more than background information and lacks interactive features. It seems odd that HSBC | www.banking.hsbc.co.uk | 1 | 0 |

| Sub Topic | Title | Description | URL | Rele-vance | Ease of Use |
|-----------|-------|-------------|-----|-----------|-------------|
| | | promotes its new TV banking service on their Web site – why not offer Internet banking? | | | |
| *ATM FINDER* | | Not much use if you're out of cash on the street, but good for planning ahead. | | | |
| | Link | Find the ATMs belonging to the Link system nearest to you, and find out which banks are members of Link. | www.link.co.uk | 3 | 1 |

## CREDIT CARDS

| Sub Topic | Title | Description | URL | Rele-vance | Ease of Use |
|-----------|-------|-------------|-----|-----------|-------------|
| *CREDIT CARDS* | | All you need to know about credit cards. | | | |
| | Caledonian Express | These licensed credit brokers specialize in services for those who've been refused credit cards. You can apply online and get useful advice on how banks operate credit-scoring systems. | www.express-finance. co.uk/personal/cards. html | 1 | 1 |
| | Credit Card Research Group | A sell for the major UK banks and building societies, who promote their industry. It does offer some useful information, but look elsewhere for truly independent advice. | www.ccrg.org.uk/ | 1 | 1 |

## CURRENCY

| Sub Topic | Title | Description | URL | Rele-vance | Ease of Use |
|-----------|-------|-------------|-----|-----------|-------------|
| *EXCHANGE RATES* | | The site below offers a simple currency converter for all your currency exchange needs. | | | |
| | Currency Converter | This is even simpler than standing in front of your local Thomas Cook; enter the value of the currency you need to exchange, choose a country, and click. | www.xe.net/map/ | 2 | 1 |

| Sub Topic | Title | Description | URL | Rele-vance | Ease of Use |
|-----------|-------|-------------|-----|------------|-------------|
| **SAVINGS** | | | | | |
| *ISAs* | | Basic information about Individual Savings Accounts and where to find the most competitive rates. | | | |
| | NetISA | This is an online service managed by Barclays Global Investors. You can invest online in an ISA and subscribe here to Tr@cker, a new online magazine offering analysis and commentary on the FTSE 100. A good site to read the latest articles about ISAs from both national papers and trade magazines. | www.netisa.co.uk/ | 2 | 2 |
| | b2 | The best site for ISAs we've come across. Offers simple-to-understand information on all aspects of the ISA, including charts detailing the different ways you can invest in these new savings accounts. You can apply for an information pack to be sent to you by post, but you probably won't need one after looking at this site. A perfect starting point for the ISA novice. | www.b2.com/ | 4 | 4 |
| | Branson's Guide to PEPs, TESSAs and ISAs | Richard Branson stamps his personality on this introductory site, which may or may not be an attraction. It seems unnecessary to describe PEPs and TESSAs after they have been discontinued, but the ISA guide is helpful, even if it seems to lead unerringly towards Virgin products. | www.isa-guide.co.uk/ | 1 | 1 |
| *PENSIONS* | | You'll find everything you've ever wanted to know about UK pensions here, whether you're thinking of getting one or you've had one for years. | | | |

| Sub Topic | Title | Description | URL | Rele-vance | Ease of Use |
|---|---|---|---|---|---|
| | Pensions Index | The site is essentially an advertisement for Lines Partnership, an independent financial management company. Its alphabetical pensions glossary, however, is a useful reference point for the beginner. | www.lines.co.uk/ index_pensions.htm | 1 | 1 |
| | DSS | Four ways to access the DSS's eight leaflets about pensions: read them on the Web; download as Acrobat files; download as text files; or phone for them to be put in the post. Whichever way you choose, the result is unbiased and valuable advice. | www.dss.gov.uk/pen/ | 1 | 1 |
| | Occupational Pensions Advisory Service | A non-profit-making advisory service that offers basic information on occupational pensions and advice on where to find help if problems arise. | www.opas.org.uk/ | 1 | 1 |
| | Occupational Pensions Regulatory Authority | The place to go to if you're having trouble with your company pension. Offers advice on who to complain to and how. Offers a pension tracing system among over 200,000 pensions nation-wide, but unfortunately it can't be done online. | www.opra.gov.uk/ | 1 | 1 |
| | Towards simpler pensions | Web site of the campaign for simpler pensions, launched in May 1999. Not much yet, but if you support the pensions charter set out on the site, you'll want to see how it develops. | www. simplerpensions. org.uk/index_e.htm | 1 | 1 |
| | National Association of Pension Funds | You'll need to become a member of this trade body for occupational pension providers for full access to its publications, but you can download the most recent NAPF policy report in full, for free. | www.napf.co.uk/ | 1 | 1 |

| Sub Topic | Title | Description | URL | Rele-vance | Ease of Use |
|---|---|---|---|---|---|
| *NATIONAL SAVINGS* | | It might have been around a while, but it's taken to the Web like 'a duck to water'. | | | |
| | National Savings | Graphics-heavy but excellent site that promotes the myriad products available from National Savings. Use the Savings Selector to assess which type of investment is best for you and click on the calculator to work out the interest you could receive from the financial product you choose. You can also find out online whether you have an unclaimed prize from your Premium Bonds. | www.nationalsavings. co.uk/ | 4 | 3 |
| **INVESTING** | | | | | |
| *INVESTING BASICS* | | Investing in stocks can be a bewildering process; most of us automatically assume that dealing in shares is for the likes of the city slickers, not for us. The sites below purport to change this misconception. They offer solid and easy-to-understand information for the first-time investor. | | | |
| | London Stock Exchange | A very useful site for the absolute beginner, impressively designed and offering advice and practical information on how to buy shares – something other finance sites rarely do. Also brings you 'Share for All', an initiative launched in 1998 to raise public awareness about how to invest in shares, plus a directory of advisers in your area. For the novice and the seasoned investor alike. | www.shareaware.co.uk | 4 | 3 |
| | The Motley Fool UK | This is the place to start for anyone interested in learning more about investing. Register for free and create your own portfolio, or enter | www.fool.co.uk | 4 | 3 |

| Sub Topic | Title | Description | URL | Rele-vance | Ease of Use |
|-----------|-------|-------------|-----|-----------|-------------|
| | | the 'Fool's school' to learn exactly what a portfolio is. Useful tips, up-to-date information and a witty, easy-to-understand approach to the mysteries of finance. | | | |
| *INVESTING RESOURCES* | | Once you've mastered the basics, move on to these sites that offer everything from the latest stock quotes (usually 20-minute-delayed for non-subscribers) to advice on your next deal. | | | |
| | Bloomberg | A comprehensive site for the investor, albeit slightly cluttered. Detailed stock quotes reveal company performance for up to a year and also provide most recent press coverage of your chosen company, though not all the articles are totally relevant. You can also access an abridged version of *Money* magazine here. | www.bloomberg.co.uk | 3 | 3 |
| | Market Eye | Offers a free investor service – simply register to access most of their features. This site keeps you up to date with the latest City financial news and prices, though you do need to pay for up-to-the-minute details. You can subscribe to their premium service for real-time data and historical information on companies. All in all, this site offers a wealth of information in an accessible and easy to navigate format. | www.marketeye.co.uk | 3 | 3 |
| | The Giltability guide | The site is produced by an investment advisory service in Taunton who are mainly interested in selling their services. Good for an absolute beginner, it offers clear and concise information and examples on all issues surrounding gilts. | www.gilt.co.uk/ | 1 | 1 |

| Sub Topic | Title | Description | URL | Rele-vance | Ease of Use |
|---|---|---|---|---|---|
| | Micropal | Standard and Poor are a mutual fund analysis company who offer free fund analysis from all major markets. Choose your market and look through a wealth of information, from fund selectors to performance tables. | www.micropal.com | 3 | 2 |
| | Daytrader | Offering company performance tips and analysis and a round-up of the day's emerging finance headlines. You can also access a UK and US IPO (Initial Public Offering) and watch offering details on upcoming IPOs. Free registration gives you access to all areas on this informative site. | www.daytrader.co.uk | 2 | 2 |
| | Easdaq | Europe-wide stock market, modelled on the highly successful NASDAQ in the US. It has a similar concentration on high-tech stocks. Small beer as yet, with only 49 companies trading at time of review. | www.easdaq.be | 1 | 1 |
| | Nasdaq-Amex UK | UK information for the NASDAQ and AMEX markets. Good section for UK investors on how to trade (you can't buy shares on this site). You can search among the 49,000 NASDAQ-listed companies, and then get a summary of whether to buy, sell or hold, from 36 stock analysts. Excellent screening function lets you find suitable companies according to your criteria. Great for the enthusiastic investor. | www.nasdaq-uk.com | 3 | 3 |
| | Interactive Investor International | A one-stop shop for all your financial needs. Find out the best-performing unit trusts and offshore funds, compare the latest online banking services, then find out the latest news on FTSE | www.iii.co.uk | 3 | 3 |

| Sub Topic | Title | Description | URL | Rele-vance | Ease of Use |
|---|---|---|---|---|---|
| | | movements. You'll also have access to financial calculators, and the day's finance news features. One of the best online financial sites we've come across. | | | |
| | In Fin Net | Glossy Web site that's striving for an up-market clientele (why offer a wine-tasting feature and a skiing guide otherwise?). It offers UK investors free Internet access. Non-subscribers have access to weekly broker reports, monthly reports on stock market behaviour, and a daily 'Top Ten Movers' from the FTSE 100 to the FTSE Fledgling. | www.infinnet.co.uk | 2 | 2 |
| *CORPORATE INFORMATION* | | These are the sites that are beginning to empower online investors to make their own choices without the need for a broker. | | | |
| | Corporate Information | A gateway to information on companies and industry throughout the world. Choose your country and you'll be provided with a list of relevant links to corporate information in that area. However, the lists are by no means comprehensive. | www. corporateinformation. com/ | 1 | 1 |
| | CAROL | Offering company annual reports online. Not a comprehensive list of all UK companies, but the information you have access to makes the trip worthwhile. | www.carol.co.uk | 3 | 2 |
| | Wright Research Center | A veritable goldmine of information on companies both in the UK and worldwide. Search the alphabetical listings of companies and you'll find performance charts over the past 5–10 years, price trend analysis and the company's latest earnings and dividends. Covers your basic needs for assessing a company's behaviour. | profiles.wisi.com/ | 4 | 3 |

| Sub Topic | Title | Description | URL | Relevance | Ease of Use |
|---|---|---|---|---|---|
| | UK Business Park | This site is subscription only but you do have access to a free three-week trial. A treasure trove of information for the serious investor – offering snippets of news on industry and company activity, including news of acquisitions and mergers, plans for business expansions and more. The site itself is simple and efficient: nothing more or less. | www.ukbusinesspark.co.uk | 3 | 1 |
| | Corporate Reports | Register free and receive summaries of company reports, or subscribe and you'll have full access to company reports of UK-quoted companies. The information here is based on excerpts from annual reports, so although the list is not comprehensive, the quality and amount of information is good. You'll need to download a plug-in for your browser to see the reports on this site. | www.corpreports.co.uk | 3 | 3 |
| *ONLINE DEALING* | | These sites offer real-time dealing, mostly on a low-commission or even commission-free basis. | | | |
| | Barclays Stockbroker | Register for real-time dealing and make full use of the Stockbrokers Price Improver – it identifies the most competitive prices around through an automatic link to major market-makers. This is a good place to start your online dealing; take full advantage of the low commission rates (at time of review). | www.barclays-stockbrokers.co.uk | 3 | 2 |

| Sub Topic | Title | Description | URL | Rele-vance | Ease of Use |
|---|---|---|---|---|---|
| | Charles Schwab Worldwide | You can deal in US as well as UK stocks here. At the time of review they offer commission-free trading for 30 days if you open an account. They're also linked with Reuters to produce a Reuters Investors Premium Service; it's subscription only but looks well worth the money – international stock coverage, portfolio tracker, online tutorials and in-depth news and views from Reuters. | www.schwab-worldwide.com | 3 | 2 |
| | E*Trade | Register for a free quote service, or subscribe in order to track company news or stock performance. A comprehensive service for the online UK stocks dealer. | www.etrade.co.uk | 2 | 2 |
| | REDM | This site offers more for free than most other online-dealing sites we've come across. You can access up-to-date searchable finance and industry news headlines, and also receive 15-minute-delayed market prices. | www.redm.co.uk | 3 | 2 |
| | Xest | An execution-only electronic share trading site, which means you don't get any investment advice. You might find this site more difficult to navigate than other online dealing sites, with bewildering links to fashion magazines and astrology charts. Disregard this and you'll find free registration to some standard features – updated finance news and stock prices, showing 5-year graphs for stock performance history. | www.xest.com | 1 | 1 |
| | InvestIn | High-quality FAQs on this execution-only share trading site. | www.investin.co.uk | 2 | 2 |

| Sub Topic | Title | Description | URL | Rele-vance | Ease of Use |
|---|---|---|---|---|---|
| | Flemings | This initially rather intimidating site actually contains a number of useful features for the potential trust investor, including downloadable documents and an attractively designed breakdown of the various investment options. | www.flemings.co.uk | 2 | 1 |
| *UNIT TRUSTS & OEICs* | | The following site will provide you with information on unit trusts and OEICs (Open-Ended Investment Companies); use it as your first stop when in the market for these investments. | | | |
| | TrustNet | A free unit trust information service. Offers daily prices and a performance league table, with a useful search facility where you can find the highest-yielding unit trusts. You can also access extensive information on investment trusts, OEICs and closed-end offshore funds, plus daily updated world indices and exchange rates. | www.trustnet.com | 2 | 2 |
| *OFFSHORE INVESTMENTS* | | In the sites below you'll find detailed information on offshore investments, for the novice and seasoned investor alike. You'll also be able to compare different funds and judge which are the best ones for you. | | | |
| | British Airways Global Financial Services | More staid and less user-friendly than some of the other sites in this area. The most recent issues of the quarterly publications *Global Money Guide* and *International Investment Outlook* are downloadable, plus the usual offshore banking services. | www.bagfs.com | 3 | 2 |

| Sub Topic | Title | Description | URL | Rele-vance | Ease of Use |
|---|---|---|---|---|---|
| | Offshore Net | An Interactive Investor International site. Use this detailed and user-friendly site as your one-stop guide to offshore banking. Once you've registered you'll have free access to portfolio and fund performance tracker facilities. Without registering you can still find an international broker or a product provider in your chosen jurisdiction. Plus access to up-to-date financial information, and the chance to share investment tips in the discussion forum. | www.offshore.net | 3 | 2 |
| | Moneynet Offshore | A good start for the offshore investments novice. If you're a complete novice, use the 'wizard' as your starting point. | www. moneynet-offshore.com | 3 | 2 |
| **MORTGAGES** | | | | | |
| *RESOURCES* | | Especially useful are the mortgage rate comparison features, which take the trouble out of collating all the information yourself. | | | |
| | MoneyNet | A free service that compares hundreds of mortgage rates after you've indicated your preferred mortgage type. Easy to use as well as extremely useful. | www.moneynet.co.uk/ | 4 | 3 |
| | Home Directory | A property and mortgage guide. You can search its database for properties, find the property of the week, and receive useful advice and information on mortgages and moving. Great links to sites that make the moving process that little bit easier, offering maps and information about local transport and local education. | www.homedirectory. com | 4 | 3 |

| Sub Topic | Title | Description | URL | Relevance | Ease of Use |
|---|---|---|---|---|---|
| | MoneyMart | A comprehensive introduction for the beginner, with the usual mortgage calculator. A clickable map gets you to a list of mortgage advisers, but you have to register and it's not very extensive yet. | www.moneymart.co.uk/mortgages.html | 2 | 1 |
| | flex-e-mortgage.com | Fill in the form and answer the questions about the type of mortgage you're after, and within seconds you're presented with a list of lenders who are most suitable for you, with details of their services. | www.flex-e-mortgage.com/ | 3 | 1 |
| | Your Mortgage | The online version of the consumer magazine. Non-subscribers have access to abridged versions of recent features, with a page devoted to updating you on the latest deals around. Calculate your monthly mortgage repayments with their mortgage calculator, and read up on a useful section dealing with non-standard mortgages if that is what you're after. | www.yourmortgage.co.uk/ | 3 | 2 |
| | John Charcol | A nationwide independent financial advisory service offering some sound basic advice. Go to the Best Buys page to find some good deals, or learn the pros and cons of differing repayment methods in the Repayments Guide. Also offers you a basic mortgage calculator and a budget planner. | www.johncharcol.co.uk/ | 2 | 2 |
| | Paragon Mortgage Specialists | You can estimate the value of your home, using regional price indices, calculate the minimum income you'll need to secure a loan, and find out how much you will need to be saving to repay an interest-only mortgage. Go to | www.paragon-mortgages.co.uk/ | 4 | 3 |

| Sub Topic | Title | Description | URL | Rele-vance | Ease of Use |
|-----------|-------|-------------|-----|-----------|-------------|
| | | the mortgage 'wizard' for a quick and easy-to-follow quote, or download spreadsheets that help you calculate useful information while offline. | | | |
| *ONLINE QUOTES* | | Online quoting services, plenty of advice, and in some cases the opportunity to secure a mortgage online. | | | |
| | Mortgages-Online | Independent advisers Burns Anderson really want your custom, but the site does offer a good deal of free advice. Helpful on how flexible mortgages work, they provide independent online quotes for your mortgage, and claim to find the best deal for your requirements. | www.mortgages-online.co.uk/ | 2 | 1 |
| | Promise | An online and telephone only re-mortgage service owned by Credit Suisse. You can fill out a form for a quick quote, or apply for a re-mortgage online and receive an answer in 10 minutes. A well-presented site and easy to navigate. Not for the first-time buyer. | www.ipromise.co.uk/ | 3 | 2 |
| | House Web | Billed as a 'property portal' this site collects resources for people buying, selling or renting property. These include information on mortgages, and a deal with ScreenTrade brings online home insurance to the site. A good place to go before the stress of moving home hits you. | www.houseweb.co.uk/house/index.html | 4 | 3 |

| Sub Topic | Title | Description | URL | Relevance | Ease of Use |
|-----------|-------|-------------|-----|-----------|-------------|
| **INSURANCE** | | | | | |
| *ONLINE QUOTES* | | The best of these sites give you competitive quotes and save a lot of phoning around. | | | |
| | The UK Insurance Centre | Choose from home, car, travel or health insurance and fill in the corresponding form to receive quotes from companies who match your criteria. An extensive form to fill out in each case, but worth it. Maintained by a panel of insurance companies who advertise on the site. | www. theinsurancecentre. co.uk/ | 1 | 1 |
| | Norwich Union | Offers online quotes for motor, home, appliances and motorcycle insurance. | www.norwich-union. co.uk/ | 2 | 1 |
| | CGU Direct | General Accident's online service. Though the site design is lacking in style, it does offer the usual basic interactive features: quotes for home, motor and travel insurance. | www.cgu-direct.co.uk/ | 1 | 1 |
| | Screen Trade | This site is owned by Misys plc, who are a supplier of electronic trading for insurance companies in the UK. It's a useful site, comparing policies on home, car and travel insurance. You can also buy the insurance policy you've chosen online. | www.screentrade.com/ | 2 | 2 |
| | Direct Line | This brash and breezy site offers quick online motor, home and travel insurance quotes and online purchase in an easily accessible form. The site provides a directory of the company's phone numbers, but you do wonder why they haven't chosen to rely more on e-mail. | www.directline.com/ | 1 | 1 |

| Sub Topic | Title | Description | URL | Rele-vance | Ease of Use |
|---|---|---|---|---|---|
| *INSURANCE COMPANIES* | | Sites that offer more than just a 'corporate brochure'. | | | |
| | UK Insurance on the Web from Taylor | A simple and comprehensive alphabetical listing of UK insurance companies with links to their Web sites and other insurance-related sites. | www.taylormade. co.uk/tmsukins.htm | 1 | 1 |
| | National Mutual | A well-produced site offering downloadable consumer guides on pensions, technical details on any insurance products, and investment reviews. No sales from the site, though: the company sells only through independent financial advisers. | www.nationalmutual. co.uk/ | 2 | 1 |
| | Equitable Life | The site offers an interactive financial planning workshop using case studies to illustrate finance options. Online service for Equitable clients who register, and information about prices and fund performance for those thinking of becoming clients. All in all a strong site, which gives relevant information and features rather than blatant plugs disguised as helpful advice. | www.equitable.co.uk/ | 2 | 2 |
| | Legal & General | Enter the interactive house on the home protection page and get advice on fire protection and safety, and insurance cover for each part of your home. There is no online quote facility, but you can e-mail a completed form, and a member of staff will get back to you with a quote in 2–5 days. | www.landg.com/ | 3 | 3 |

| Sub Topic | Title | Description | URL | Rele-vance | Ease of Use |
|---|---|---|---|---|---|
| *CAR INSURANCE* | | Most have online quotes for car insurance; some sites let you buy online as well. | | | |
| | Autobytel | Read the advice on buying and selling cars, decide which car you're interested in, then type in your postcode and find your nearest car dealer. Also advises on buying or selling used cars. Links to Bank of Scotland and Alliance & Leicester provide calculators, which assess how much you can afford to pay and how much you need to borrow. Finally, links to CGU and Eagle Star advise you on your motor insurance. A one-stop site for the car-owner. | www.autobytel.co.uk/ | 3 | 3 |
| | Norwich Union | Online quotes available on this straightforward site. | www.norwich-union.co.uk/ | 1 | 1 |
| | Car Source | Claims to find the cheapest quotes and the best cover from over 450 insurance schemes. You can choose from two forms; the first will be sent to a group of five insurers who will then e-mail you a quote; the second will get you an online indication of what your insurance may cost you. | www.carsource.co.uk/ | 1 | 1 |
| | Car Quote | This site allows you to get quotes from 11 insurance companies by filling in a single form. A nice idea, because filling in online forms can get really tedious. No instant quotes, though, and you have to phone each company to follow up your request. | www.carquote.co.uk/ | 1 | 1 |

| Sub Topic | Title | Description | URL | Rele-vance | Ease of Use |
|---|---|---|---|---|---|
| **TAXATION** | | | | | |
| *TAX ESSENTIALS* | | If you're having trouble filling in your self-assessment form, or need to know which tax bracket you're in, have a look at these sites. They offer basic information about taxes that we all need to know. | | | |
| | ThomTax | Aimed mainly at the tax professional, it gives clear information on everything from capital gains tax rates to VAT and Inheritance Tax. Essential information but it could benefit from a more imaginative interface. | www.thomtax.co.uk | 1 | 1 |
| | Inland Revenue | Not the most imaginative site you'll ever see, but it has lots of information on tax issues. Being able to download forms is a particularly handy feature. | www.inlandrevenue. gov.uk/home.htm | 2 | 2 |
| | Chartered Institute of Taxation | This straightforward site helpfully lists two main categories: tax for beginners and tax for experts. | www.tax.org.uk | 2 | 2 |
| | Tax Tips | Though this is essentially an advert for an independent firm in Bournemouth, it does offer basic tax advice via an attractive book-style layout. | www.taxtips.co.uk | 2 | 3 |
| | Line One | Some interesting articles such as '10 ways to make money', plus a Dr Tax and Dr Mortgage who answer your tax and mortgage questions. Useful and fun site. | www.lineone.net/ money/ | 3 | 3 |

| Sub Topic | Title | Description | URL | Rele-vance | Ease of Use |
|-----------|-------|-------------|-----|------------|-------------|
| **FINANCIAL NEWS** | | | | | |
| *NEWS SERVICES* | | Up-to-the-minute global news from the world's most reliable sources. | | | |
| | News Now | The latest financial news updated to the last 5 minutes. You don't even need to register for this formidable service. Search the latest articles by industry or by topic, in the US and the UK, and read the full article online. This is a well-designed and highly useful site for keeping up to date with financial affairs. | www.newsnow.co.uk/ | 3 | 4 |
| | Moreover | A daily round-up of finance headlines throughout the world. This site gathers headlines from 1,500 sources that are searchable by industry or country. | www.moreover.com/ | 1 | 1 |
| | Reuters | Offering a world news service via a not terribly well-thought-out site. Go to the site map to locate the information you require. | www.reuters.com/ | 2 | 1 |
| *NEWSLETTERS* | | You'll find information in these specialist financial newsletters that is difficult to find elsewhere. | | | |
| | Small Cap Review, EASDAQ Investor, The AIM Newsletter | All three newsletters are available from this site by subscription only. You can download recent samples from each one, and decide whether it's worth paying for. | www.newsletters.co.uk | 3 | 1 |
| | Financial News | The subscription-based online version of the London weekly. The paper offers in-depth coverage of European and international finance issues for the seasoned investor and finance professional. | www.financialnews.co.uk | 1 | 1 |

| Sub Topic | Title | Description | URL | Rele-vance | Ease of Use |
|---|---|---|---|---|---|
| | Fuller Markets | Web site of a monthly newsletter from global strategist David Fuller. Offers daily market analysis, trading strategies and charts for the stock market, commodities, currencies, interest rates and bonds. You can get three back issues free to help you decide whether it's worth the money for the basic newsletter or the premium service with additional fax and e-mail updates. A daily forecast on a particular topic is also free. | www.fullermarkets.com | 2 | 2 |
| *ONLINE NEWSPAPERS* | | Look through these sites for the best of the online versions of daily national finance-oriented newspapers. The most interesting ones offer features above and beyond their printed counterparts. | | | |
| | Observer business | Business and finance news brought to you from the *Guardian* and *Observer* newspapers. You can log in as a guest for 24 hours, but after that you'll need free registration. | www.newsunlimited. co.uk/business/ | 2 | 2 |
| | Financial Times | This is the *Financial Times'* free site. No need to subscribe, but you will need to register for the global archive, portfolio and news by e-mail services. You'll also find specialist areas such as FTEuro, together with daily market news and updated prices. | www.ft.com/ | 3 | 3 |
| | Electronic Telegraph City and Finance | A section of the *Daily Telegraph's* online edition. Click on City and Finance and you'll see today's stories, but if you want to read them you'll need to register free of charge. | www.telegraph.co.uk/ | 2 | 1 |

| Sub Topic | Title | Description | URL | Rele- vance | Ease of Use |
|---|---|---|---|---|---|
| *ONLINE MAGAZINES* | | Most of the online magazines are available on a subscription basis only, but you do have access to abridged versions in some cases. | | | |
| | The Economist | Register to gain access to an abridged version of the current issue. To get an article from the searchable archive you'll need to spend 1 credit (=$1) from the 5 free credits you get on registration. | www.economist.com/ | 2 | 2 |
| | Business Week | Only subscribers to the print edition get free run of this site, but even so there is a great deal of free material to keep you abreast of (mainly US) economic developments with a special focus on the Internet. | www.businessweek. com/ | 3 | 3 |
| **ETHICAL FINANCE** | | | | | |
| *ETHICAL INVESTING* | | Ethical investing is gaining popularity with the advance of environmentalism and an increasing sensitivity to ethical issues in politics. Converts and sceptics alike will find something to interest them here. | | | |
| | UK Social Investment Forum | Find out which banks, building societies and lenders are socially responsible institutions and why. A basic site that is good for the investor who is approaching ethical investment for the first time. | www.uksif.org | 4 | 1 |
| | Shared Interest | A co-operative lending society, which lends your money to Third World small businesses. It's a simple and straightforward site that also contains a useful list of producers to whom your money is going. | www.shared-interest. .com | 1 | 1 |

| Sub Topic | Title | Description | URL | Rele-vance | Ease of Use |
|---|---|---|---|---|---|
| | The Ethical Partnership | Independent financial advisers for ethical investing. Take a look at their list of ethical funds available in the UK, complete with the latest rates on offer. Also a good place to start to find out exactly what an ethical fund means, to you and the provider. | www.the-ethical-partnership.co.uk | 1 | 1 |
| *ETHICAL BANKING* | | Banks with attitude. | | | |
| | Co-operative Bank | You'll find a detailed description of their ethical policies, plus highlights of the many campaigns they support, on this site. See Online Banking for their Internet bank called smile. | www.co-operativebank.co.uk | 3 | 2 |
| | Triodos Bank | An ethical bank with a simple Web site. You may need to phone them to get more detailed information. | www.triodos.co.uk | 3 | 1 |

# Index

# About Illustra Research

Illustra Research was formed in January 1999 to develop products and services that would make the Internet more effective and easier to use for everyone. Their mission is to put the power of the Internet within easy reach of both novice and experienced users alike.

Located in the Sussex Innovation Centre at the University of Sussex, UK, it is supported by a network of specialists and experts in the UK and the USA who cooperate on specific projects, using the Internet as a collaborative tool. Illustra also employs teams of researchers who surf the Web to locate relevant material. They are managed by Web Editors, who work alongside subject specialists to rigorously evaluate information according to a unique methodology.

The directors of Illustra:

Alan Saunders, Managing Director, has been in the multimedia industry since its birth and has worked on projects for a wide range of blue-chip clients including Hewlett Packard, Olivetti, British Airways, NEC and Panasonic.

Colin Dixon, Technical Director, has worked with computer networking systems and PC technologies for over 15 years.

Alan Cawson, Research Director, is Professor of Digital Media and Director of the Digital Media Research Centre at the University of Sussex. He has been involved with the Web since its birth in 1993, and writes extensively on consumer information technologies.

For further information about Illustra's activities please contact:

Illustra Research Limited
The Sussex Innovation Centre
Science Park Square
Falmer
Brighton BN1 9SB
Tel: 01273 234650
e-mail: info@illustra-net.com

# How to Use Your Top 200 CD-ROM

The CD-ROM that accompanies this book runs under Windows 95, Windows 98 and Windows NT4.0. It is a combination of a high-quality information directory and a fully featured Web browser. The information directory is a guide to the Internet, in which relevant sites are identified, and ordered by topic and sub-topic. Each site has been evaluated for relevance and ease of use according to systematic criteria. Integrated with the directory is a Web browser engine, Microsoft's Internet Explorer, providing seamless integration with the Internet. The browser provides all online features of Internet Explorer, so the user is not 'missing' any functions available to users of other browsers.

1 Topic Index   One-click access to links organized within topics and sub-topics using drop-down menus which helps users move quickly to the subject area they wish to research.

2 Browser Window  The user sees entries in the directory in the browser window, and with a   single click can navigate to the relevant Internet site.

3 Toolbar  A clear toolbar provides one-click access to key functions, including Back, Forward and Print. A special 'Guide' button returns the user immediately to the directory – saving time and providing instant help when 'lost' on the Internet.

4 Menu Bar  A standard Windows Menu Bar contains all the functions of the CD-ROM.

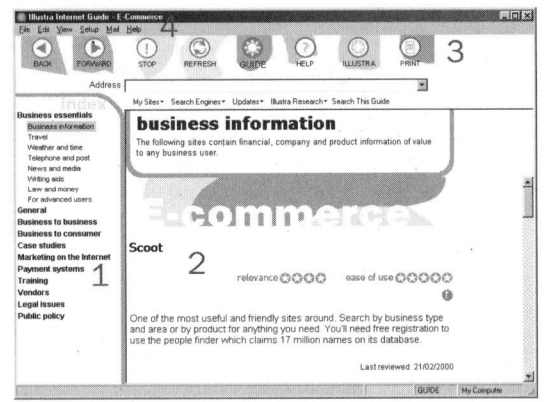

## Installation

The CD-ROM installs easily on the user's hard disk. The user can choose where it is installed. Full uninstallation is provided.

## Online Update

The Internet is changing all the time as sites appear, change or close down. The CD-ROM includes an update feature, through which users can connect directly to the Illustra Web site, and download an updated version in a matter of seconds.

## System Requirements

| PC System | Memory (RAM) | 16 Mbytes minimum |
|---|---|---|
| | Disk Space | 20 Mbytes required |
| | CD-ROM | 4x required |
| | Operating System | Windows 95, Windows 98, Windows NT4.0 (Service Pack 3 or later) |
| Display | Minimum screen resolution | 800x600 |
| | Minimum screen colour depth | 15-bit (32768 colours) |
| Online Requirements | Internet Connection | Windows dial-up or LAN connection to Internet provider |
| | Modem | Any supported Windows modem |
| | Microsoft Internet Explorer | Optional. The Guide will supply Internet Explorer functions where IE is not installed, and will upgrade IE versions 1–4 to IE5. |